PETER KINNELL

More Erotic Failures

Futura

A Futura Book

This edition published in 1985
by Futura Publications, a Division of
Macdonald & Co (Publishers) Ltd
London & Sydney

ISBN 0 7088 2836 1

Typeset, printed and bound in Great Britain by
Hazell Watson & Viney Limited,
Member of the BPCC Group,
Aylesbury, Bucks

Futura Publications
A Division of
Macdonald & Co (Publishers) Ltd
Maxwell House
74 Worship Street
London EC2A 2EN
A BPCC plc Company

For all the guys at *Time Out* magazine,
in particular, John Diamond,
the inspiration for this book.

'It is the foolishest act a wise man commits in all his life.'

Sir Thomas Browne

'Certainly I find the climax immensely exaggerated.'

Virginia Woolf

'The whole story is told in bed.'

Leo Tolstoy

CONTENTS

CONTENTS

INTRODUCTION

With the publication of this book, the work of the Institute of Erotic Failures, Flops and Libido Loss – the EFFALL Institute as it's now known – reaches a most interesting stage.

Over the past two years, the Institute has been inundated with reports of an intimate and embarrassing nature from around the world – adulterers from France, kinky dentists from Holland, weird exhibitionists from the home counties, South American nymphomaniacs, dodgy Israeli gynaecologists, irrepressible premature ejaculators from all over the United States, Irish voyeurs, German celibates and, of course, practically every erotic failure conceivable from South Africa.

As the evidence poured in, it has been the duty of my researcher, Miss Jenny Prior, and myself to check each flop and failure in its turn. Many's the occasion when Jenny and I have found ourselves working late into the night, verifying each story, eager to bring our researches to a conclusion that is satisfactory for us both.

The international flops included in this volume and its predecessor *The Book of Erotic Failures* have enabled us to establish a few tentative guidelines as to the quintessential nature of erotic failure – in particular, the sort of person it is most likely to strike, and the form in which it is likely to appear. Feeding each story into the EFFALL computer, we have come up with the following basic research data:

Top Twenty Most Common Causes of Erotic Failure

1. Underenthusiasm (male).
2. Bizarre stimulants required.
3. Underenthusiasm (female).
4. Disastrous honeymoons.
5. Misguided beliefs about the birds and the bees.
6. Overenthusiasm (male).
7. Caught in the act of being unfaithful.
8. Excessive devotion.
9. Overenthusiasm (female).
10. Exhibitionism.
11. Compulsive self-abuse.
12. Swaps that back-fired.
13. Over-affection towards animals.
14. Worries over size and/or performance.
15. Unfortunate loss of virginity.
16. Nymphomaniac mothers-in-law.
17. Chronic sexual boredom.
18. Mental cruelty (female to male).
19. Unfortunate elopements.
20. Excessive fondness for marriage.
20. Erotic encounters with an alien.

Top Twenty Professions Most Likely To Be Affected By Erotic Failure

1. Policemen or women.
2. Writers.
3. Rock singers.
3. Priests.
5. Actors.
6. Prostitutes.
7. Doctors (esp. gynaecologists).
8. Actresses.
8. MPs.
10. Kings.

*Priests, spies, disc jockeys, air hostesses, politicians,
hookers, ballroom dancers, rock singers, poseurs, moral
crusaders, con men, nurses, pornographers, judges,
strippers, choirmasters . . .*

The heroes of this book have little in common beyond
the fact that each of them, in his or her bizarre way,
has been spectacularly, humiliatingly, sometimes
even historically unsuccessful in matters of love and
lust.
Just when it was all beginning to go well, suddenly
things started to go very, very wrong . . .

Also by Peter Kinnell in Futura:

THE BOOK OF EROTIC FAILURES

11. Stars of sex films or stage acts.
11. Journalists.
13. Judges.
14. Hippies.
15. Soldiers.
16. Air hostesses.
17. Nuns.
18. Disc jockeys.
19. Judges.
20. Emperors.

Other Professions Quite Liable To Suffer from Erotic Failure

Queens, sultans, academics, dentists, undertakers, sexologists, nurses, ballroom-dancers, eunuchs, popes, publishers, spies, diplomats, saints, tax inspectors, lorry drivers, pornographers, postmen, comedians, milkmen, traffic wardens, choirmasters, village idiots, footballers, opticians, moral crusaders, thieves, librarians and jockeys.

Conclusions

1. Apart from members of the police force – whose propensity for sexual oddities of almost every type were in a class of their own – the professional spread of erotic failures recorded by the computer was quite close. Priests, for instance, were only a few points ahead of actors and prostitutes, yet the sheer quality of their flops lifted them a couple of places in the charts. Disc jockeys, on the other hand, turned in a disappointing result and were only kept in the Top Twenty by a brilliant all-round performance by the 'Romeo of the turntables' Tony Blackburn. I have taken the liberty of docking a few points off journalists because they all lie so much.

2. The EFFALL computer was unable to come up with a final conclusion about the geographical distribution of erotic failures, beyond establishing that those which fell under the general heading 'Underenthusiasm' more often than not came from the United Kingdom, Sweden, Italy and, surprisingly, Australia. Otherwise the spread of erotic failures was fairly even, although compulsive self-abuse featured prominently in reports from the United States and West Germany.

3. These figures are not the last word. There is an ongoing programme within the EFFALL computer that is ceaselessly assimilating information as it reaches us. If you feel, while thumbing through this volume, that you may have experienced erotic failures that are considerably more embarrassing than any in this book, we need your evidence urgently. So please send all details – under a plain wrapper, if possible – to me at the EFFALL Institute, c/o Futura Publications, for consideration in future volumes.

On the other hand, you could simply consult a reputable doctor.

Peter Kinnell, 1985
EFFALL Institute

ONE

TOO UNLUCKY

'Greatest horror – dream I am married
– wake up shrieking.'

J. M. Barrie

MOST EMBARRASSING LEGAL MISUNDERSTANDING

The principle defence witness in a rape case, Mrs June Bolger, when questioned as to what the accused said to her before the rape, replied that the words were too strong to be said out loud in court. The judge agreed that they should be written down and showed to members of the jury.

When the man sitting next to fellow jury member Hazel Willing passed her the written note, he found he had to nudge her to wake her up. Taking the note, Mrs Willing read it, smiled and put it into her handbag. Asked by the judge to show it to other members of the jury, Mrs Willing refused on the grounds that it was too personal and had nothing to do with the case.

LEAST ADVISABLE LOVE-PLAY FOR ENGAGED COUPLES

The *Sunday People*'s 'Dear Barbara' column recently revealed an unusual problem. After watching some boxing on the television, wrote 'Sharon', she challenged her fourteen-stone fiancé Bob to three rounds in the lounge diner. In the first round, she gave Bob a playful tap on the chin – and he keeled over unconscious. When he had come round, Bob begged her never to spar with him again.

'I love him very much but this has got me worried,' wrote Sharon. 'How can I respect a husband whom I can beat up physically?'

LEAST GALLANT IRISHMAN

After a prostitute calling herself Lulu found the young Samuel Beckett asleep on a park bench in Dublin, she took him home and looked after him – in every way – for several weeks. Then she started to complain – Beckett never did anything but loll around the flat, and anyway she was pregnant with his child.

'She kept plaguing me with *our* child,' he wrote later, 'exhibiting her belly and breasts and saying it was due at any moment, she could feel it lepping already. "If it's lepping, I said, it's not mine." '

He left the next day.

LEAST AFFECTIONATE WIFE

'This was not exactly a spur-of-the-moment crime of passion,' said the prosecuting counsel at the trial in San Diego of Carol Hargis for the murder of her husband David, a Marine drill instructor.

The court heard how, after she had insured his life to the tune of $20,000, Mrs Hargis and a friend called Mary Depew had decided to kill him. They first of all searched some nearby woods for a rattlesnake and, having failed to find one, returned with a tarantula, which they served up in a pie. David said it was 'revolting' and refused to eat it.

Subsequently the two women tried to electrocute him in the shower, poison him with lye, run him over with a car, get him to hallucinate and possibly kill himself by putting over fifty amphetamines in his beer (he wouldn't drink it) and inject his arm to put a bubble in his bloodstream (the needle broke).

A plan to leave a number of bullets in the carburettor of his truck was shelved, when Depew pointed out that she wanted to have the truck after his death. Finally they opted for beating him over the head with a 6½ lb weight while he was asleep. It worked.

WARMEST LOVER'S LEAP

A honeymoon on the romantic volcanic Reunion Island went badly wrong for newlywed Philip Ryan. Returning to his bride after a midnight stroll, he vaulted the fence which he believed surrounded the honeymoon home and fell straight into the crater of the Ganga Volcano.

MOST PROBLEMATICAL NOSE

'To begin with she is magnificently ugly – deliciously hideous,' wrote Henry James about George Eliot. 'She has a low forehead, a dull grey eye, a vast pendulous nose, a huge mouth, full of uneven teeth, and a chin and jaw-bone *qui n'en finissent pas.*'

Eliot's looks became something of a legend in Victorian literary circles. Herbert Spencer claimed that he had once been in love with her but the affair had foundered because her long nose made kissing impossible.

Later in Eliot's life, she received a bizarre proposal

from a German professor. He wrote that he had just seen a photograph of her and wanted to marry her – for some time, he had been looking for a wife who could both translate from German and who was impressively ugly. Sensing a joke, Eliot wrote back, enclosing the most hideous photograph of herself that she could find.

The professor wrote back quickly, saying that he had to withdraw his offer since she was not quite ugly enough.

LEAST IMPRESSIVE FIRST DATE

On journalist Dave Banks' first date with a new girlfriend, all went well until he visited the restaurant loo. When he emerged, his shirt tail was inextricably caught in his zip, leaving four inches of shirt hanging out.

'I returned to our table at the double – a 6ft 5in fella looking like Groucho Marx playing the Hunchback of Notre Dame. Back at her place, my trousers caught fire when I tried to burn the shirt tail out of the zip and I got quite a nasty scorching!'

Mr Banks now works for the *Sun*.

SILLIEST SULTAN

Early Muslim leaders guarded their womenfolk jealously, and no more so than the second-century sultan, Qutb-ud-din of Gujarat. One day the sultan decided to show his many wives around the capital city of Ahmedebad and issued an order that no man should be seen on the streets. As the royal party toured the town, the sultan spotted a young boy on a street corner looking at the procession. In a fury, he struck out at the boy with his sword, but missed and struck his own knee. He died a week later from the wound.

SHORTEST-LIVED APOLOGY

Mrs Jane Robinson was deeply upset when her husband insisted that a blood test should be carried out on their fourth child because he bore no resemblance to him.

After the test brought the good news that all four children had the same father, Mrs Robinson demanded an apology. Then she revealed the bad news – all four had been fathered by Mr Robinson's best friend George Bryant.

MOST EMBARRASSING NAMES

While it is rare that a name alone can constitute an erotic failure, John Train, the author of *Remarkabilia*, has discovered a number of genuine cases which should be included on the grounds of the lifelong embarrassment they have caused:

Dr Beaver, obstetrician
Cinderella Hardcock, art student
Mr Clapp, venereal disease counsellor
Mr Cock who married *Miss Prick*, according to *The Times* of 1963
Dr Fealey, gynaecologist
Mustafa Kunt, Turkish military attaché
Le No Fuck Bébé, a French swing band
Love Nookey Good, a nurse
General Plastiras, a Greek politician of whom Winston Churchill once expressed the hope that he did not have 'feet of clay'
Needa Climax, Methodist church officer
Oral Love, nursing home proprietor

WORST NEWS FOR BALLCRUSHERS

An early Babylonian law decreed:

'If a woman has crushed a seignior's testicle in a brawl, they shall cut off one finger of hers, and if the other testicle has become affected along with it by catching the infection, even though a physician has bound it up or she crushed the other testicle in the brawl, they shall tear out both her eyes.'

IMPOLITEST PRIMATE

While making love on the banks of the River La La, Mr and Mrs On Madai soon found they were not alone.

'We had just begun,' said Mr Madai, 'when an ape rushed out of the jungle and raped me from behind. I did my best to drive him off but he was very persistent and, having knocked me to the ground, he then raped my wife.'

In spite of his wife's objections that 'it was only a monkey', Madai reported the ape's behaviour to the local police.

DULLEST MR PLOD

In the early 1950s, the legendary advice columnist Abigail van Buren received the following poignant letter:

'Dear Abby

I am a lonesome policeman, 36 years of age, and I have always lived with my mother. She passed away and I would like to get married, but everybody tells me that I am foolish to look for a wife because these modern girls are not the type to give you three hot meals a day. All I want is a nice girl who will go to Church with me on Sundays and give me three hot meals a day. Is that asking too much?

Larry the Lonely Policeman'

While a number of readers responded in a sensibly dismissive tone ('Dear Abby, Larry the Lonely Policeman must have rocks in his head. He doesn't want a wife – he wants a mother. No thanks. Bonnie'), a surprising number of them agreed with Abby's verdict that 'if all you want is three hot meals a day, I'd say you were a pretty hot prospect.'

Oddest of the lamebrains who responded enthusiastically to Larry's letter was the following:

'Dear Abby

I would like to meet Larry the Lonely Policeman. I am considered an excellent cook and think it's a woman's duty to fix her husband three hot meals a day. And even more if he wants it. I also go to Church.

Ella C.'

MOST INCONGRUOUS HONEYMOON COUPLE

There was good news and bad news for Stephanie, the bride of Bristol shopowner Timothy Taylor. The good news was that, in spite of the pressure of work at the shop, the honeymoon would still go ahead. The bad news was Timothy's mother would be taking his place.

'It may be unromantic, but that is the way I am,' Taylor told a local reporter.

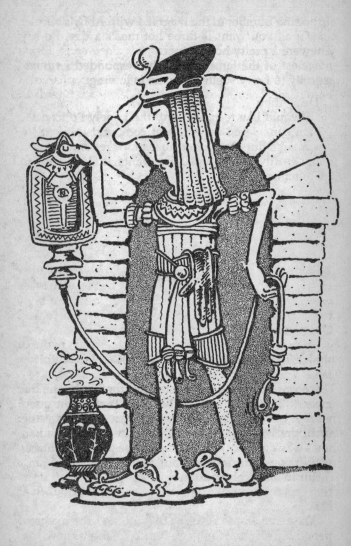

LEAST DESIRABLE COURT APPOINTMENT

The popularity of enemas, fully documented in *Forum* magazine, is nothing new. In ancient Egypt, enema-makers were privileged members of the pharaoh's entourage. They rejoiced in the title of 'Shepherds of the Anus'.

MOST RAPID PUBLIC DEFLATION

Truman Capote and Tennessee Williams were in a bar in Key West when a woman, slightly the worse for wear, approached their table. She was wearing a brief halter top and, holding out an eyebrow pencil, asked Capote to autograph her belly button.

He refused but Williams happily signed his name in the required place and the woman returned to her table. Then her husband appeared on the scene.

'Before we knew it,' Capote recounted later, 'he had grabbed the eyebrow pencil out of her hand and walked over to where we were sitting, whereupon he unzipped his pants and pulled out his cock and said to me – "Since you're autographing everything today, would you mind autographing *mine*?"

'I had never heard a place with 300 people in it get that quiet. I didn't know what to say – I just looked at him.

'Then Tennessee reached up and took the eyebrow pencil out of the stranger's hand. "I don't know that there's room for Truman to autograph it," he said, giving me a wink, "but I'll initial it."'

NASTIEST SHOCK FOR MRS WARD

Michael Ward of York admitted that he had done his best to murder his wife because frankly he couldn't stand the sight of her. Mr Justice Jupp, presiding over the case, took a sympathetic view and sentenced Ward to two years probation.

'You are a danger to no one except your wife,' he said.

RUDEST INTERRUPTIONS OF THE MARRIAGE CEREMONY

In the state of Kerala in India, the chief priest had the right to enjoy the favours of any newly wed bride before she joined her husband and even the ruler of the province was forbidden to make love to his new wife before the priest had enjoyed her for three days.

For one Brahmin sultan, the onerous duty of deflowering other men's wives became something of an obsession. Humayin Shah Brahmin handed over administration of his state to deputies while he pursued these more personal affairs of state. So keen on this procedure was he that the sultan developed the habit of halting any wedding procession that he saw and taking the bride back to the palace for his personal pleasure, sometimes only returning her to her distressed husband days later.

26

TWO

TOO UNPROFESSIONAL

'Police passionately love victimless crimes because they can extort money from prostitutes – not to mention the odd blow job.'

Gore Vidal

SWIFTEST ABOUT-TURN IN POLICE HISTORY

A policeman was said to have made 'an unprofessional proposition' when he caught an attractive police-woman breaking the 30 mph speed limit in her car. But when the woman unbuttoned her tunic to prove that she was a stripogram artiste in her popular 'WPC 69' outfit, the police constable withdrew his suggestion and booked her on the spot.

The girl was fined £38 for speeding.

WORST SIDE EFFECTS OF TOO MANY EROTICO-GYMNASTIC ACTS

'I just didn't know what I was doing,' Miss Yvonne Bullen, a blue movie star, told police after she had been arrested for shoplifting. 'It has been nothing but work, work, work for the last two years. In over thirty sex films, I have performed over two thousand erotico-gymnastic acts. You can see I am dazed by it all because the goods for which I forgot to pay were all dog foods and I poisoned my alsatian Casanova by mistake last week.'

Miss Bullen later told a court that she had given up her acting career and hoped to get into the undertaking business.

BEST CASE OF GAMESMANSHIP

After twenty-five year old girl jockey Lee Custance won on the 20–1 outsider Regal Segment at the Port Lincoln track in Australia, she was called in to see the stewards. There she was told that, by wearing excessively brief bright red knickers, she had influenced the result of the race. The other jockeys had been so mesmerized by Lee's back view that none of them had been inclined to pass her.

Following her victory and the subsequent publicity, Lee said she had been offered a large number of their rides.

STUFFIEST CORRESPONDENT

When Evelyn Waugh received an unusually gushing fan letter from a married woman, he expressed his gratitude by sending the letter to her husband with the following note:

'I regret to inform you that your wife has entered into correspondence with a strange man. I return to you her letter, which she imprudently wrote me. I trust you will administer to her whatever form of conjugal chastisement is usual in your part of the USA.'

Yours
Stuffy Waugh'

KINKIEST CHRISTMAS ENTERTAINMENT

The *Observer*'s listing of seasonal entertainments for the Christmas of 1967 contained the following item:

> 'SOOTY'S XMAS. Harry Corbett with his hand up that little bear again. MAYFAIR THEATRE.'

MEANEST QUEEN

Queen Anula, wife of King Coranaga of Ceylon led an eventful life. Historians have reported that she grew tired of Coranaga early in his reign and poisoned him. Shortly afterwards, she fell in love with a palace guard, who became King Tissa when they married. Unfortunately, soon after the marriage another palace guard called Shiva caught the queen's eye. She appointed him first Palace Watchman and then king – after she had first poisoned Tissa. Shiva was poisoned in his turn as were his successors, King Damala Vatuka, formerly a carpenter, King Namudi, formerly a woodcutter, and King Niliya, a Brahmin.

Niliya was to be Anula's last husband. After he had reigned for six months, the queen poisoned him because, according to the history books, she was lusting after all thirty-two of the palace guards.

Queen Anula then took the throne herself. She had reigned for only four months when her subjects, tired of her ridiculous behaviour, overthrew her and had her executed.

31

MOST UNUSUAL CHORAL TECHNIQUE

Parents of schoolgirls in a local girls' choir became alarmed at the unconventional training methods they received, a Sussex court has heard. The part-time choirmaster had told some of the girls to come to his house for 'microphone aptitude tests'. There he placed them, blindfolded for fullest concentration, in front of a large board with a hole in it, through which he said, he would be holding the microphone. The girls were than asked to practise what he called 'close mike technique.' But, the court was told, it was not a microphone that was used.

The man was found guilty of gross indecency.

MOST RIGOROUS IN-DEPTH INTERVIEW

Interviewing Miss Angelika Flach for the position of dental nurse in his surgery, Mr Peter Hepton, a dentist from Lancaster, explained to her that his most successful operations had been performed when his assistant wore long black boots and suspender belts.

He then asked Miss Flach to wrestle with him on the floor in order to test whether she was suitable for the job.

'I wanted to see if she had the strength to handle patients coming out of anaesthetic,' he later told a court.

BUSIEST NECROMANCER

Although the sixteenth-century celebrity Simon Forman had no conventional qualifications as a doctor, his skill as an early alternative physician earned him a huge fortune, as well as some significant side benefits.

His professional specialities included metroscopy (the reading of the lines on the face), astrology, necromancy and the solution of marital problems; his personal ones revolved mainly around what he called in his diary 'halek'. The entry for 9 July 1607, when he was fifty-five, read, 'Halek 8 am Hester Sharp, and halek at 3 pm Anne Wiseman, and halek at 9 pm Tranco (his wife)'.

Forman's love of halek did not go entirely unnoticed. The Royal College of Physicians announced that he was a 'mountebank and a charlatan', after one Frances Howard, who had been suffering from 'night flutterynges of the heart', had described her treatment. 'He devoided me of my nyght-gowne and, having given me a potion to drive out devills, soothed me upon my breasts until I was plees'd.'

While the doctor's love potions were regarded as being unharmful during his lifetime, this opinion was revised after his death. Forman died from the affects of one of his specially prepared aphrodisiacs in 1611.

MOST GRATUITOUS MENTION OF THE SEX ACT IN A FOOTBALL REPORT

From the *Irish News and Belfast Morning News*:

> 'Last time out the Armagh boys accounted for Castleblayney and the wide open space of Omagh will suit their style of play. It promises toben aeentr   fuck it   to be an entertaining game, which could go either way.'

ANOTHER VERY GOOD REASON NOT TO TRUST DOCTORS

The sloppy habits and general carelessness of members of the medical profession extends beyond the surgery into their private lives, it has been revealed in the *British Journal of Sexual Medicine*. While more than half of the doctors in Britain have received specialist training in family planning, over a third take no precautions whatsoever when making love.

SILLIEST SOVIET SEXOLOGIST

In his book, *Sex in the Soviet Union*, Dr Mikhael Stern, a Russian endocrinologist who defected to the West, managed to summarize the sexual nature of the entire Russian population in a few words:

'Sexual technique is generally very poor. The woman has little experience and is very passive. The man is unskilful, often brutal and quick. Often he imagines that the penis need only penetrate the vagina for the woman to be immediately overwhelmed with happiness. If this does not happen, he becomes angry or depressed . . . After ejaculating, he hurriedly dismounts, turns over and falls asleep.'

The word 'orgasm', Dr Stern reveals, is a 'foreign import, only used by doctors. Almost the only term in everyday language is virtually untranslatable, the verb *konchat*: literally 'to finish', which is a truly sad comment on sexual relations.'

Dr Stern's views on Western sexuality, from which the popular verb 'to screw' is almost untranslatable into Russian, have yet to be published.

MOST COMPREHENSIVELY BROKEN VOW OF CELIBACY

A Portuguese man living in Brazil during the fifteenth-century was convicted after it was discovered that he was the father of 299 children by 59 women, including his own mother, 5 of his sisters, 29 adopted daughters and 3 of his slaves. Incest was not unusual at the time but the fact that Father Fernando da Costa was the local Catholic priest may have influenced the judge. He was found guilty and imprisoned.

TACKIEST POLICE PROCEDURES

According to an article in *Company* magazine, the professional body with the highest rate of erotic failures is the police force.

'It's a man's life, I can tell you that,' former police-woman Kate Burgess said. 'From the beginning of my training, I realized that a woman was sneered at if she did well in exams. The men couldn't believe that a woman could do better than them.'

Burgess went on to reveal that sexual harassment has become part of police procedures, with clumsy seduction attempts taking place on night shifts and constant pressure on policewomen to sleep with superiors to gain promotion.

'The way they questioned prostitutes about the seedy side of their work before letting them go was pathetic and disgusting. They just wanted to hear about the sex.'

Burgess' revelations are borne out by a report published by the Policy Studies Institute which compared the values of the force to those of 'any all-male institution, such as a rugby club or boys' school'.

The former policewoman also revealed that bizarre initiation ceremonies attend the arrival of female 'probationers' at each station.

'New policewomen were grabbed by the men, their knickers pulled down and their bottoms printed with the station's rubber stamp. There's nobody to complain to. All the sergeants and inspectors joined in.'

Asked to comment, a Scotland Yard spokesman replied that 'the alleged bottom-stamping incident' would be investigated.

GRUMPIEST BROTHEL-KEEPERS

The outbreak of the Black Death in 1349 caused such a sense of panic and disenchantment with religion that throughout Europe ancient pagan rites and devil-worship were enthusiastically revived. Sexual frenzy reached its peak with the creation of special establishments in villages and towns, designed for nude bathing and orgiastic pleasures.

Although brothels were busier than ever before, there were still complaints from brothel-keepers – they were apparently receiving unfair competition from convents.

WORST CASE OF THE SNOOPER SOCIETY

After a photographic developing firm had sent some photographs of a man's wife in her bath to the local police, a spokesman for the firm pointed out that they like to vet the moral content of film sent in by the public for developing. 'When in doubt we like to check with the authorities,' he said. 'We're not too strict – in general, topless pictures of wives and girlfriends are entirely acceptable.'

THREE

TOO DIRTY-MINDED

'I am much too interested in other men's wives to think of getting one of my own.'

George Moore

MOST ENTHUSIASTIC POLICE UNIT

A nurse from Copenhagen was bundled into a police van in Soho after the local constabulary had made one of their customary raids on a peep show. Protesting that she had been in the audience with her boyfriend, she was told by police that she had been arrested 'because she looked like a stripper'. The investigating officer then asked her if she was wearing any knickers.

OBSCENEST ACADEMIC

Shocked by the bad language of one of the lecturers, a group of female students in the anthropology faculty of Cambridge University decided to take action. They wrote the man a note, warning him that the next time he used 'obscene, demeaning or sexist language' in a lecture, there would be a walkout of all the female students present.

The man opened his next lecture with the words 'The men on the Polynesian island of Loti are said to have the biggest pricks in the world.'

Without a word, the girl students closed their notebooks and made for the door. As they were going, their lecturer shouted after them, 'No hurry, girls – the next plane doesn't leave till Saturday.'

MOST STIMULATING INTRODUCTION TO THE SEX-AND-VIOLENCE AGE

'It is bad enough having to rear a daughter in this sex-and-violence age without her being obliged to sit on the lap of this or that boy in order to get a seat on the school bus,' said Mrs Winifred Saucy of Burnham-on-Crouch when asked why she was complaining about overcrowding on the way to and from school.

'I would not be complaining if the bus drove over decently surfaced, straight roads. But round here the lanes are very bendy and full of bumps. The children are going up and down all the time.'

LEAST INTELLIGENT SEXPIONAGE TECHNIQUES

The sexual revolution appears to have passed by the Mr Plods of international intelligence in London and Washington. Anxious to counter the successful Soviet deployment of so-called 'sexpionage' techniques, they set to work to perfect ways of trapping and blackmailing the enemy by the deployment of high technology and low cunning. In order to gain material that would be useful in getting Ivan over to our side, they tried the following intimate bugging devices:

1. A tiny microphone attached to the back of a bluebottle, which would be gassed at the critical moment. This was dismissed as being 'cumbersome and impractical'.

2. Pills that transmitted a signal from the stomach. Both the spy and the target would, it was argued, have swallowed a signal-transmitting pill and, when

their two bodies were close to one another, the signals would coalesce. At that moment, the camera boys could jump in. 'Technical problems' in the consumption of the pills caused this plan to be abandoned.

3. A microphone concealed in a fake nipple of the (presumably female) spy. In a trial run a prototype for this method came adrift under 'oral pressure' and was thought to be too risky.

4. Cameras fixed into the framework of the bed. But then on several occasions the 'target' preferred to make love on the floor or in the bath and the cameras missed all the action.

5. A transmitter fitted into the vagina that would be triggered by 'chemical changes'. Two problems here: firstly, the chemical changes failed to occur within some of the cooler spies. And then there was the problem of oral and other forms of sexual activity which 'bypassed the normal channels'.

So it was back to the drawing board in Whitehall and Washington.

EARLIEST EXAMPLE OF TALKING DIRTY AS AN ESSENTIAL PART OF FOREPLAY

Historians have discovered that Mesopotamian women used mystic incantations when their menfolk were suffering from impotence or sexual exhaustion. Among the most popular were: 'Let a horse make love to me', 'Let his penis be a stick of martu wood', and more confusingly, 'Let his member strike the anus of the woman'.

MOST REGULARLY PRACTISED FIRE DRILL

Officials from the union COHSE have been asked to investigate why administrators at a London hospital regularly insisted on letting off smoke bombs late at night in a nurses' home. The hospital claims it is part of a routine fire practice but the nurses have another theory: prurient officials were trying to flush out boyfriends sleeping in the nurses' quarters.

LEAST SUCCESSFUL TALK WITH GIRLS

The Victorian obsession with the appalling evils and dangers involved in self-abuse was not restricted to boys – girls had to be on their guard as well. In his book *Talk With Girls*, E. B. Kirk wrote:

'There is one thing, however, which may most seriously hurt a girl's body, and that is touching the private parts in any way to make the sensitive nerves a sensation of pleasure. Sometimes schoolgirls do this out of ignorance or curiosity, but they run the risk of hurting themselves for life through it. A tired dull feeling is often the result the next day and sometimes even nerve affections may be started which injure the brain.'

Older girls appear not to have taken Mr Kirk's advice too seriously. A medical journal of the time reported the following list of items found about the person of women patients: cucumbers, bananas, candles, turnips, beetroot, pencils, sticks of sealing-wax, cotton-reels, hair pins, knitting needles, compasses, glass-stoppers, toothpicks, toothbrushes and eggs.

BEST EXPLANATION FOR CITY BEHAVIOUR

'Red is the colour of sex, yellow is the nerve energizer that keeps us awake. Our bodies and minds will drive in different directions. Everyone knows that you cannot make love and think at the same time.'

Miss Eloise Barnhurst, a colour consultant from Cape Cod, propounded this theory while explaining that new amber street lights in the town would have a disastrous effect on the townspeople's morals and sexual stability. When asked for more positive proof, Miss Barnhurst said: 'I once drove past a motel with amber lights in Washington. I wanted to scream, throw rocks, dance naked and copulate, all at the same time. But I managed to restrain myself because I am seventy-three.'

ODDEST AWARD

The International Association for Eroticism which, according to *Forum*, has been set up 'to encourage people in the sex business to take a pride in their profession', has made its first award. The IAE Award for an imaginative promotion has been given to *Penthouse* magazine for their selling slogan 'IT'S WELL 'ARD'.

48

THE PLAY LEAST LIKELY TO BE REVIVED BY THE NATIONAL THEATRE

A dramatic comedy described by the *Dictionary of National Biography* as being 'of intolerable foulness' was performed before the court of Charles II in 1684. Entitled *Sodom or the Quintessence of Debauchery*, it told the story of Bolloxinon, the King of Sodom, who orders Borastus, his Bugger-Master General, and his deputy Buggeranthos, to decree throughout the kingdom that the only sexual activity permitted henceforth would be – you've guessed it – sodomy. Among the other characters in the play were: Cuntigratia, the Queen, Prince Pricket, Princess Swivia and her four maids of honour, Fuckadilla, Officina, Cunticula and Clytoris.

MOST BELATED CORRECTION

From the *Dagenham Post*:

'In a report last week of a court case involving Edward Brien of Scottes Lane, Dagenham, we wrongly stated that Mr Brien had previously been found guilty of buggery. The charge referred to was, in fact, burglary.'

SILLIEST CASE OF COITUS INTERRUPTUS

When police in Gillingham were alerted by a midnight call from a man who heard a burglar sawing his way into a nearby house, they were round with two cars and five police constables within minutes. After a lengthy search, they found two copulating hedgehogs under a bush. The police separated them and the sawing noise stopped.

MOST COMPREHENSIVE CODE OF CONDUCT

Religious texts written in Britain during the fifth and sixth centuries reveal a complex system of penances for sexual misdemeanours. Among the punishments recommended by *The Synod of the Grove of Victory* and *The Book of David* were:

Adultery – a three year penance
Incest with mother – a three year pilgrimage
Fornication with a nun – a lifetime penance
A Bishop who fornicates – a thirteen year penance
   (the same as murder)
Bestiality – a two-and-a-half year penance
Sodomy – a four year penance
Masturbation – a two year penance
A seminal emission – seven psalms on rising and
   bread and water for a day
Self-touching – twenty-four psalms on rising

SILLIEST CASE OF SEXUAL JEALOUSY

The fact that D. H. Lawrence became impotent relatively early in his life caused him untold misery and frequently caused him to react with an irrational fury to apparently minor incidents. His friend Knud Merrild witnessed a bizarre scene in Lawrence's back garden. Seeing his pet dog Pips merrily coupling with a neighbour's mongrel, 'he kicked and mauled the pet within an inch of his life'.

Merrild was obliged to separate 'the tortured dog and the absolutely insane author'.

UNLUCKIEST SUNBATHER

Two policewomen were commended by a magistrate for their determination and courage in tackling a middle-aged married man who wanted to sunbathe in his underpants, the *Manchester Evening News* reported. Harrop and Barker spotted Mr Alan Dzlegel in the act of taking his trousers down on St Anne's sandhills and had pursued him eagerly for some time before Miss Barker dragged him to the ground with a flying tackle. Before he could put his trousers on, Miss Harrop slapped a pair of handcuffs on him.

Complimenting both women for playing their part in the fight against crime, the magistrate found Dzlegel guilty of indecent exposure and gaoled him for three months.

MOST SPECIALIZED SMALL ADS GUIDE

Among the most useful terms included in the glossary of the *Sex Maniac's Diary 1985* are:

'SWT' or 'switchable' – can be either dominant or submissive
'W/E' – well-endowed
'T/T' – tit torture, breast bondage
'A–Z' – willing to abuse, talks dirty
'Roman' – likes orgies
'Animal training' – likes bestiality
'Hobbyist' – likes amputees

BEST EQUIPPED TOURING NOVELIST

In her normal frank no-holds-barred interview, on this occasion with *Playboy* magazine, Erica Jong likes to reveal that she travels around with a collection of diaphragms in her briefcase. She also carries penicillin tablets with her 'because I have the greatest clap phobia of anybody in the world'.

MOST DIRTY-MINDED INTERPRETATION OF A RELIGIOUS TEXT

Many interpreters of the Koran believe that it allows only one sexual position. Their evidence is the words, 'Cursed be he who maketh woman Heaven and himself earth.'

FOUR

TOO CLEAN-MINDED

'I'd rather drink than diddle.'

H. L. Mencken

MOST MISGUIDED MORAL CRUSADE

In September 1975, *The Times* reported on a bizarre chain of events in London's Hyde Park:

'Paul Delprat was painting by the Serpentine when he observed a woman take a duck from her shopping bag and put it in the water to lure the drakes. As the drakes approached the woman snatched them, wrung their necks and tossed them in the litter baskets. When Delprat remonstrated the woman rounded on him: "There are too many drakes in the world," she cried. "They are raping the ducks, the owls and even the swans." '

MOST PANIC-STRICKEN NEWLY-WEDS

When Maithrey Mohan of Orpington got married at the age of twenty-seven, she had never been told the facts of life. But since her husband-to-be was thirty-one, she was confident that he would have a basic grasp of the rudiments.

He didn't. At two o'clock in the morning of their first night together, Maithrey had to wake up her parents to ask them what they were meant to do. After a brief lecture, the couple returned to bed to try again.

MOST HYGIENIC LOVE CULT

Disciples of Bagwan Shree Rajneesh were surprised by instructions that awaited them when they arrived at the Master's 64,000 acre ranch in Oregon for a love festival. The Master, who has for some years advocated free love among his followers, was worried that the spread of new sexually transmitted diseases might make him the leader of the most heavily contaminated cult in the world.

Taking swift action, he ordered disciples to avoid kissing each other. He also handed out specially blessed rubber gloves and contraceptives which were to be worn at all times of sexual contact.

MOST EMPHATIC SECOND THOUGHTS

Sexual activity appears to have been held in low esteem among intellectuals in the early seventeenth century. In his *Religio Medici* of 1642, Sir Thomas Browne wrote:

> 'I could be content that we might procreate like trees, without conjunction, or that there were any way to perpetuate the world without this trivial and vulgar way of union: it is the foolishest act a wise man commits in all his life.'

Sir Thomas loosened up later in his life, got married and, presumably with conjunction, fathered ten children.

ODDEST INTERPRETATION OF WORDS BY ALFRED, LORD TENNYSON

Novelist and oddball Ernest Hemingway was fond of quoting Tennyson's dictum, 'Old age hath yet his honour and his toil' in support of his own pet sexual theory. He believed that each man had an allotted number of orgasms in a lifetime and that he should therefore pace himself extremely carefully.

SADDEST SWAPPER

Agony aunt Marge Proops was unsympathetic when a male correspondent described his problem. One evening, he and his wife had visited a married couple with whom they were friends. Towards the end of the evening, his wife had disappeared into the garden with the other man and they had been discovered by the man's wife making love behind the woodshed.

Far from being embarrassed, the adulterous couple forced Marge's correspondent and the other woman to complete the swap by having an affair.

'She agreed because she is terrified of her husband. I agreed because I felt it would be insulting to this woman to refuse,' the reluctant swapper explained. 'It is very difficult because there is no real desire and she is nearly always in tears anyway. But my wife and her partner are happy as Larry.'

Marge told him to grow up.

MOST EASILY SHOCKED EGYPTIANS

'This could give serious offence to the citizens of Cairo,' said the British Council when asked why ten seconds had been cut out of an educational film about budgerigars. The ten seconds concerned how the budgies reproduce.

GLUMMEST HONEYMOON

'I think that the erotic element in her was faint and tenuous,' wrote Quentin Bell about Virginia Woolf. Certainly her marriage to Leonard Woolf appears to have done little to enliven her interest in sex. A few days after the couple had left for their honeymoon, she wrote to Vanessa Bell, 'Why do you think people make such a fuss about marriage and copulation? Why do some of our friends change upon losing chastity? Possibly my great age makes it less of a catastrophe; but certainly I find the climax immensely exaggerated.'

She was thirty at the time.

HIGHEST PRICE PAID FOR SEXUAL MODESTY

A man in Tokyo hit on an original way of relieving pure-minded shop-keepers of their takings. While the owner of one luggage shop, Miss Kikuko Hattari, was emptying the till at the end of a busy day, the man walked in, took down his trousers and gave her a full frontal flash. Miss Hattari screamed and turned away. The thief grabbed the money and walked out, zipping himself up.

STRONGEST REASON FOR NOT DATING MORMONS

'He seemed a nice bloke, attractive in his T-shirt and jeans. I agreed to show him the English countryside the next day,' said Maureen Danvers of Luton. 'But he turned up wearing a bright blue Crimplene suit, a shocking-pink shirt and a Russian hat, like a refugee from a vodka advert.

'Then he started cleaning the car and singing "The Hills are Alive with the Sound of Music" at the top of his voice. I was too embarrassed to be seen with him in public so I took him home to meet my Mum. I had told her that he was a Mormon and her first words were, "Hello, I hear you're a moron."

'I left the house when he started reading the Bible at my Dad while he was trying to watch racing on the telly.'

MOST RADICAL EDITORIAL PROPOSAL

The British publisher of Jacqueline Susann, pioneer of the sex 'n' drugs 'n' high finance school of fiction, was shaken to the core when the manuscript for *Valley of the Dolls* came in and suffered something of an erotic failure of nerve.

He sent a cable to the author, which read: 'I WOULD LIKE YOUR CONSENT TO CUT OUT F—K THROUGHOUT THE BOOK IF YOU CAN AGREE WILL GREATLY INCREASE SUCCESS EMPIRE MARKET STOP.'

He received a reply the next day: 'F——K YOU. LOVE. JACKIE SUSANN.'

Nonetheless, the f—s were finally taken out of the British edition.

MOST TYPICALLY BRITISH EXPORT

Raising 'as a matter of some urgency' the question of how chastity belts should be taxed, Mr Marcus Lipton MP told the House of Commons in 1971. 'It seems absurd that foreigners can buy these belts without tax, but the British husband or father who wants to protect his wife or daughter has to pay extra.'

The case had reached the Commons after the Anne Huggessan Organization, which did a roaring trade in belts based on a medieval design, had asked the Customs and Excise office whether they should be subject to purchase tax. The answer came by return – the men from the ministry had determined that chastity belts were articles of clothing and therefore the tax should be paid.

Lipton's question in the Commons resulted in a climbdown by the civil servants and, as a result, five thousand of the belts, which weighed two pounds, had a nine month guarantee and came with two keys (the second one being for the bank manager), were sold during 1971.

The firm were so inundated with orders at one stage that it had difficulty meeting the demand – particularly since several of the women making chastity belts were reported to be taking maternity leave.

STRONGEST ARGUMENT AGAINST KNICKERS AND FRENCH LITERATURE

The author of the dubious work *Mysteries of Verbena House*, which was published in 1882, had some invaluable advice to women troubled by lascivious thoughts.

'The greatest enemy to a woman's chastity is contact,' he wrote. 'Let her wear her things loose, and she may keep her blood cold. Nuns – continental ones at least – don't wear drawers.'

But without doubt, the greatest danger to virtue was caused by 'wearing corsets while reading French novels'.

PROUDEST EDUCATIONAL ACHIEVEMENT

'All 25 girls in the sixth form are still virgins,' announced Mrs Weila Noko MA at the Tumutumu Girls School end of term ceremonies to applause from the assembled parents.

'Not one of my girls has dropped out through

pregnancy. I know my suggestion to put bars across dormitory windows found little favour when it was suggested. But the sugar-daddy mad girls used to leap out like flies into tomato soup. Nowadays, if they arrive intact, they leave intact.'

MOST RELUCTANT VOLUPTUARY

After a lifetime of wild and licentious behaviour, Louis XIV was thought to have undergone a conversion when he married Madame de Maintenon, a deeply religious woman who had once been governess to the king's children. Mme de Maintenon tried to reform the king and save his soul but had little success. Although she tried to enter into the spirit of things at the court of the Sun King, she had herself bled twice weekly to avoid blushing at the lewd behaviour and salacious gossip of the courtiers.

WORST NEWS FOR LITERARY NECROPHILIACS

A book called *Naboth's Vineyard* by Jonathan Latimer, published during World War II, was found to dwell so lovingly on the joys of necrophilia that it was banned and copies ordered to be taken from the publisher's warehouse and burned by the public hangman. The book's most famous line was said to be, 'Gee! Only one woman a year, and that a dead 'un!'

CRUELLEST GRANDMA

'Dear Abby

I am 69 but I still like the ladies. When my "old lady" suspects that I am going out without her, she hides my false teeth. I don't do much harm but I like to get out alone once in a while. What should I do?

Granpa Max'

MOST SURPRISING RELIGIOUS HEADGEAR

There was confusion and embarrassment in literary circles soon after Robert Browning's poem 'Pippa Passes' was published. The lines that caused the trouble were:

'Then, owls and bats,
Cowls and twats,
Monks and nuns, in a cloister's moods,
Adjourn to the oak-stump pantry.'

According to all known sources, the word 'twat' had come into use some time in the seventeenth century and had only one meaning: the female pudendum. Yet when the editors of the Oxford English Dictionary wrote to Browning to ask in what sense he was using the word, the poet impatiently replied that a twat was a headgear used by nuns.

As Eric Partridge later put it, this was 'a hair-raising misapprehension – the literary world's worst brick.'

THE LESSER KNOWN STRUGGLE OF THE LADY WITH THE LAMP

Throughout her life Florence Nightingale was wracked by feelings of guilt about masturbation. In her diary of 15 March 1850, she wrote, 'God has delivered me from the great offense and the constant murderer of all my faults.'

But a few days later, she had suffered from a relapse. 'My enemy is too strong for me,' she wrote. 'Everything has been tried.'

FIVE

TOO WEIRD

'I've often thought that I would like
To be the saddle of a bike.'

W. H. Auden

LEAST FASHIONABLE WAY OF TELLING YOUR FORTUNE

According to Sir Richard Burton, several tribes in Africa had a novel way of testing whether fortune will smile on a man. If he managed to catch a female crocodile, flip it over on its back from which position it is said to be helpless, and copulate with it, then he was guaranteed success in later life.

LEAST ROMANTIC HUSBAND

King Ibn Saud of Saudi Arabia once boasted that he had four hundred wives but had never seen the faces of any of them.

STICKIEST FREAK-OUT

Describing what he calls the 'Suck philosophy', writer and sexual liberationist Heathcote Williams has revealed the beautiful scenes in which he and other ageing hippies were involved in the early 1970s:

'Beauty fucked the Beast. The beautiful people had to fuck twenty ugly people before they could fuck each other, and then when they'd fucked twenty ugly people, they didn't know their arsehole from breakfast time, and all the aesthetic cobwebs were blown away, and everyone was a beautiful fuck. Love is the highest form of energy that we are capable of transmitting and fucking is sparking the physical gap of orgonic wind, so that the human molecule is cohesive and strong and eternally expanding, and the world can be changed for the best fuck it's ever known.'

Williams sums up this bizarre scene with the words, 'Everyone was lovely, and suddenly the vision of everyone Coming Together could only be physical . . . no longer intellectual.'

LEAST SUBTLE CON TRICK

A herbal doctor from Imo, Nigeria, Mr Aba Owerri, had an unusual and lucrative sideline. He would walk up to people, ask them to shake his hand and, as they did, he would fall to the ground crying out that his genitals had vanished.

As the victims recoiled in confusion, members of Owerri's gang rushed up and robbed them.

Local authorities decided to take drastic action. They handcuffed the doctor to the back of a Land Rover and paraded him around the town with his genitals exposed. Owerri, the local people were told, was in no way lacking, as they could now see. He was, in fact, the father to 114 children, over a half of whom helped him to rob innocent citizens in this way.

COUPLE WITH THE ODDEST TASTE IN MEN

Grinning disc jockey Tony Blackburn has written at length about his many sexual conquests and in particular an 'amazing evening' he spent with 'Diddy' David Hamilton.

'These two girls came over to us in a restaurant,' Tony recalls. 'One put her legs on the table so we could see she wasn't wearing any knickers. Not to be outdone, the other girl exhibited her generous bosom.'

Amazing!

MOST RADICAL HEALTH AND BEAUTY COURSE

It was in the early sixteenth century that the Countess Elizabeth Bathay reached the difficult age. Her husband died in 1604 and she was alone in her castle deep in the Carpathian mountains. At the age of forty-three, she was afraid that her looks were fading and that she would be unable to find a suitable young lover to take her husband's place.

Luckily, she was versed in the black arts. One day, in the course of duty at the castle, she had cause to slap one of the servant girls around the face, drawing blood. To her astonishment the hand on which the blood was spilt looked somehow younger than the rest of her body. Could it be that the blood of virgins could rejuvenate her? It was worth a try, she decided.

The Countess and a gang of hand-picked servants took to combing the countryside for virginal young girls. They would be captured and brought back to the castle, where they would be hung up in chains and drained of their blood. Every day, the Countess would bathe in blood, and drink it with her supper.

After five years, it became clear that this course was not having the desired effect. So, believing that the blood of upper-class girls was more beneficial, the Countess set up a sort of finishing school for the daughters of the local gentry at the castle. Then she finished them.

News of this antisocial behaviour finally reached the Hungarian Emperor Matthias II and the Countess was brought to trial in 1610, accused of the murder of no less than six hundred girls.

While her accomplices were burnt as witches, Countess Bathay, being of noble birth, was locked up in a small room in her castle where she died four years later.

ODDEST LOVE SACRIFICE

In order to prove how much he loved his wife, Mr Dan Rubbage of Alberta, Canada deep-fried their pet gerbil Oscar and, while the couple visited the local Eatery Feedery, substituted it for her baked chicken.

'The morning after she discovered Oscar on a bed of chips, she left the house,' Rubbage told the *Calgary Herald*. 'I had no intention of swindling the Feedery. I only wanted to sue them to prove how much I love Gaylor.'

LEAST PUBLICIZED ASPECT OF THE CREATIVE PROCESS

Anthony Burgess provided a surprising insight into the private life of the creative artist, when he was interviewed by *Playboy* magazine. 'I think most artists find that when they're writing something, they become sexually excited. But it would be a waste of time to engage in a full-dress – or undress – sexual act with somebody at that moment. So they often go into the bathroom to masturbate. (Dylan) Thomas did that all the time. Quite a number of artists masturbate when they write. Our sexual energy has been aroused, now we come, now we're able to concentrate on the other aspect of this energy, which is the creative aspect.'

Now if you'll just excuse me for a moment . . .

KINKIEST *YORKSHIRE POST* AD

'Successful businessman widower seeks affectionate understanding female to shave the enjoyable things in life.'

LEAST SUBTLE MEDICAL TEST

A solution to the herpes problem for the average lecher has been proposed by an unnamed denizen of New York's singles bars. Having found her man for the night, she allows him to relax in bed while she caresses his palm. Then, when his defences are down, she rams her thumb down on his pulse and says briskly, 'You've got herpes, haven't you?'

'If his pulse jumps, he's out of the door within seconds,' she says. 'If he just laughs, I know we can swing in safety.'

LEAST LIKELY SOURCE OF QUESTIONS FOR JUNIOR POP QUIZ

Charles White's *The Life and Times of Little Richard* provides some unusual insights into the lifestyle of a rock n' roll superstar. Among Richard's favourite offstage activities were masturbation ('Everybody used to tell me that I should get a trophy for it – I got to be a professional jacker-offer . . . seven, eight times a day'), various forms of homosexuality ('You know how I got gay? My momma wasn't paying attention at the time. You know, if she'd said "homosexual" when I was a little boy I wouldn't have known what she was talking about') and, above all voyeurism ('They should have called me "Richard the Watcher" ').

Early in his career, Little Richard's penchant for watching other men – massively endowed in the trouser department, if possible – make love to his girlfriends landed him in gaol. While driving a young friend called Dorothy, plus male attendants, around in his car – 'she'd be in the back of the car, the lights on, her legs open and no panties on' – Mr Rock n' Roll made the mistake of driving into a gas station. The petrol pump attendant took one look in the back of the car and called the police.

More recently, Little Richard has become a born-again Christian – although his sermons are unlikely to get him invited to contribute to 'Thought for the Day'. Here he is on his favourite, and possibly his only, theme:

'All of you secret sinners and closet folk, I'm gonna tell you. So you won't have to go back in the closet. I'm letting you stay out tonight. You can just lock it up and throw away the key. Some of you that has been shackin', you can just go packin' . . . God never intended me to go with nobody but a woman. I don't care what I get cut off. I don't care what I add on. I don't care what I get sewed to. In Heaven, my name is still Richard Penniman. I may call myself Marie down here, but in Glory, I'm still a man.'

Little Richard has an explanation for why this version of the gospel is so rarely heard: 'Some preachers don't preach it, 'cos they'd lose their whole choir. Some of 'em don't preach it 'cos they'd have no pianist and no organist! No lead director and no lead vocalist . . . Don't you forget, the Devil himself was a master musician.'

LEAST ROMANTIC LONELY HEARTS QUEST

The personal columns of the *East Africa Standard* in December 1975 included the following:

'Nanyuki farmer seeks lady with tractor with view to companionship and possible marriage. Send picture of tractor. Littlewood. Box 132, Nanyuki.'

LEAST SAVOURY PRIVATE PHYSICIAN

One of the many mysteries surrounding the life and death of Adolf Hitler is how a greedy, ill-washed and unqualified eccentric called Theodore Morrell came to be the Fuhrer's personal physician from 1936 to the end of his life.

'Professor' Morrell had established a reputation as a 'specialist in intimate diseases' by travelling around Germany on a tricycle and holding 'consultations' in a booth that he would erect himself beside the tricycle. He was photographed by Hitler's official photographer, became well-known and was one day summoned by the Fuhrer himself. He travelled to the Chancellery on his tricycle, flanked by uniformed SS outriders on motorbikes.

It is unlikely that he won Hitler over with his personal charm – he was described at the time as being 'fat and grubby, cringing in manner, and with small pig-like eyes that glittered with greed behind thick pebble glasses'. He did however discover that the eczema from which Hitler thought he suffered was, in fact, advanced syphilis and it was probably this secret knowledge that kept him in the Fuhrer's employ for the years to come.

Since Hitler was a serious hypochondriac – flatulence, insomnia, fear of impotence and body odours were among his obsessions – there was a constant demand for Morrell's pills, which included 'anti-gas' medication, cocaine and extract of bull's testicles. Critics of 'the Professor' were speedily despatched to concentration camps and soon he was prescribing his dubious medicines to most of the top-ranking Nazis.

Some believe that Morrell's pills speeded Hitler's physical decline. No less than twenty-eight different types of pill were found scattered around the Fuhrer's room after the assassination attempt in 1944. In fact, the 'Professor', who kept his job through a bizarre form of sexual blackmail, may have helped the Allied cause no end.

BRAVEST FLASHER

A school visit to the bear pit at London Zoo was interrupted recently when a man jumped into the pit, dropped his trousers and invited two Russian bears to dance with him.

'No one will stop me flashing,' Mr Kynham Dudley shouted as he was taken away by police.

London Zoo's bearkeeper Mr Bob Tuffy commented, 'Rusty and Jumble just walked away. They were disgusted.'

LEAST HICCUP-PRONE POET

Like many authors, Baudelaire believed that, for a writer, orgasm was evil and the trap of the devil. In his *Advice to Writers*, the poet suggested that only prostitutes or hideously ugly women made suitable wives for the serious artist or intellectual, and the women particularly to be avoided were 'the virtuous wife, the blue-stocking and the actress'.

'Generally speaking,' he concluded, 'The mistresses of poets are ugly sluts of whom the least bad of the lot are those who know how to cook up a decent soup and turn over their money to another lover.'

Baudelaire was however fascinated by women, and in particular the way they looked and smelt.

His mistress of twenty years Jeanne Duval would visit him regularly and give herself over to his sexual gratification. This involved sitting in a chair for a few hours while her lover gazed at her in silent adoration.

'He was not undersexed, not truly a virgin poet,' wrote his biographer Alex de Jonge. 'He simply felt there were greater pleasures to be derived from sex than the hiccup of orgasm.'

DOTTIEST AYATOLLAH

As Imal Banu, a carpenter, and Fatima Taleba, a prostitute, were hurrying through the streets of Tehran on the way to her flat for a spot of non-revolutionary activity, they were seen by a public-spirited citizen and taken to the local Revolutionary Committee. When the evidence was presented to him, the Ayatollah Quha disbanded the trial, having first declared the couple man and wife. Mr and Mrs Banu should lead a holy life from henceforth, he decreed.

GRIMMEST SEX MANUAL

Dr Zalkind's *The Revolution and Youth*, published in 1925, established the basic ground rules for doctorially correct sexual behaviour in the Soviet Union. He stipulated that:

1. The sexual act should not take place too often.
2. One should not change partners frequently.
3. Love should always be monogamous.
4. During the sexual act, one should always beware of the possibility that a child may be conceived.
5. Sexual choice ought to operate according to class criteria and ought to conform with revolutionary and proletariat goals.
6. The class (i.e. the Communist Party) has the right to intervene in the sex life of its members.'

Summing up, Zalkind explained that 'sexual attraction for someone belonging to a different, hostile and morally alien class is a perversion of the same order as sexual attraction towards a crocodile or an orang-outang.'

PHONIEST MR SEXY-BOY

'I noticed that he was quite well developed but nothing out of the ordinary in my experience,' said beauty queen Joan Pewsey, one of the judges at the controversial Morecambe Mr Sexy-Boy beauty contest. 'I awarded him third prize.'

Miss Pewsey had been asked for her comments after one of the contestants, Charles Moorcroft, had been found to be carrying a large power-drill down the front of his Union Jack bathing trunks.

Despite his explanation that he carried the drill around with him for security reasons, Moorcroft was disqualified and banned from appearing in future Mr Sexy-Boy competitions.

MOST FLAWED SOLUTION TO A LITTLE DOMESTIC TROUBLE

'Dear Abby

My husband and I have been having a little domestic trouble so I finally got him to go to a marriage counsellor with me. We were advised to take an interest in each other's hobbies. Well, I'm trying, but it makes me sick to my stomach to go down to the city dump and shoot rats. My husband gets into training for deer hunting this way and this is how he spends every spare minute. Am I supposed to go along and join him in this sport, do you suppose? I haven't got the heart for it. Please advise me.

"No Shooter" '

FICKLEST TREE-LOVER

Asked by Police Constable Moskyn Broadway why he had been shouting and hitting a tree before falling to his knees and smothering its roots with kisses, Mr James Piplow replied that he had nothing against trees in general but had been on bad terms with this particular oak for several weeks.

MOST REVEALING USE OF
PHALLIC IMAGERY

Psychiatrists in Italy believe that they have come up with a reliable test for the sexual character of their female patients. They ask them to draw a tree – any tree.

Among the most significant results are:

A wind-swept tapering cypress
She is unconventional and sexually insatiable, bordering on nymphomania.
A small Christmas tree
She is afraid of men and sex and is likely to be happiest with a small and sexually undemanding partner.
A weeping willow
She has strong lesbian inclinations.
A billowing elder or lime tree
She sees sex as no more than a means to having a house and family security.

A short stocky oak
She has a normal, healthy appetite with no orgasmic difficulties.
An anonymous-looking shrub
She has little or no interest in sex and may be frigid.

A pilot scheme involving men patients drawing lakes and mountains was reported to have been less successful.

MOST UNUSUAL SOURCE OF
SEX APPEAL

After he had photographed the Prime Minister, photographer Norman Parkinson startled attendant journalists by saying that of all the beautiful women he had photographed, Mrs Thatcher had the most sex-appeal.

Writing in the following week's *Mail on Sunday*, Jilly Cooper was in full agreement. 'She looks great – not a day older than when I last saw her. The turned-down, airforce-blue eyes are as bright as ever. The blonde hair more ashy and corn-coloured.'

'Extremely pretty,' Jilly concluded, 'not unlike Selina Scott's rather serious blue-stocking sister. She's Maggie-nificent!'

LONELY HEART MOST LIKELY TO REMAIN LONELY

A small ad from *City Limits* magazine:

> If you are sickened and angered by what you see around you: people who have sought the security of chains, whose lives are testaments to daily cowardice, and who are slaves to social constraints that have but one purpose: to tame and to peddle the narcosis of 'conventionality'; and if you believe there are no utopias on earth; and that only cretins and corpses are uncomplicated, then I would like to meet you if you are a sensitive, alert, discriminating woman. Be courageous, behave unexpectedly. Do not abuse your time – it will not be returned to you. Nietzsche said 'live dangerously'. Please help me to do so, for 'the hour is getting late'. Box E179.

HAPPIEST END

After a twenty-year-old man from South Carolina had his penis chopped off by a butcher's knife wielded by his lover's husband, the organ and its owner were taken to Atlanta Emory University Hospital. Six hours after the incident, the man was reunited with his penis after a three hour operation. A few weeks later, the man reported that it was as good as new.

SIX

TOO GOOD FOR THEIR OWN GOOD

'An Englishman in a state of adultery
is miserable: even at the supreme
moment his conscience torments
him.'

Hippolyte Taine

MOST NAIVE STARLET

David Niven liked to tell the story of a somewhat naive young actress whom he once took to dinner with a Hollywood director well-known as a groper. The man lived in a large house off Rodeo Drive which was guarded by an enormous Great Dane.

Niven noticed that both she and their host, who was sitting next to her, had communicated very little throughout the meal – in fact, his young friend had seemed flushed and ill at ease.

On the way home, he asked her if she had enjoyed the dinner. She replied that she had 'except for that awful dog'.

Puzzled, Niven asked what had happened.

'I mean, throughout the meal . . . its nose was . . . I mean, right *up* my skirt and sort of . . . probing, you know – I just didn't know what to *say!*'

Nor did Niven. The dog had been locked up before dinner began.

MOST INNOCENT FOOTBALLER

During England's 1984 tour of South America, one of the top footballers returned to his hotel room to find his room-mate and fellow team member involved in an intimate off-the-ball incident with a local girl.

He enquired as to his chances later and the girl told him it would cost him $200. Seeing that the Englishman was losing interest, she added, 'Or you score me some coke'. The footballer eagerly ran to the nearest soft drinks dispenser and hurried back with a can. The girl left in disgust.

THICKEST HUSBAND

An item from the lawcourts correspondent of the *Philadelphia Enquirer*:

' "Because my husband and I had not been getting along for some time," said Mrs Geraldine Toro, "I hired a man to blow him and his car up; but this went wrong. Then I got my friend John Kotch to ambush him outside a Pizza shop, but John got tangled up in a tree. After that, a friend of Elizabeth, my daughter, offered to do the job for $25. Bob – that's my husband – was asleep. Elizabeth turned him over in his sleep so that her friend, Harry, could get a good shot. Well, he lived, and afterwards we were discussing what to do with the body when Bob appeared at the top of the stairs and asked what was going on.

"It was very embarrassing. We sent him back to bed and gave him a lot of sleeping pills but nothing did any good. Then a friend of Bob's tipped him off, to the fact that I wanted him out of the way.

"After that, someone told the police and I was arrested. However, Bob has put up $50,000 bail and we are now entering our nineteenth year of married life." '

MOST TOTALLY MIND-BLOWING POST-MARRIAGE FREAK OUT

There was rejoicing among the beautiful people when film-maker and alternative guru Dennis Hopper married the singer from the Mamas and the Papas, Michelle

Phillips. Although the couple had lived together for some time, Dennis felt they should marry in order to bring stability to Michelle's career. Eight days after the marriage, she left home to work with Leonard Cohen.

Dennis rang her. 'I love you, I need you,' he said.

'Have you ever thought of suicide?' was the reply. It was the end of a really beautiful scene.

LEAST RANDY WEST COUNTRY VILLAGE

An ambitious scheme to revive the traditional feast of Randy Day has had to be abandoned through lack of interest.

When the Reverend David Pennal from Hardfoot, Dorset, was told about how Randy Day used to be celebrated with much rushing about with Randy Poles and rolling in the hay, he excitedly championed its revival and ordered special Randy Poles to be built.

'In the old days, the girls were only supposed to surrender after a Randy Pole touched them,' he said, 'but we live in more permissive times. It is anybody's guess what will happen.'

But the locals failed to respond to the trendy vicar's idea and Randy Day once more fell into abeyance.

BEST LEGAL PROTECTION FOR SADISTS

Until the late nineteenth century, it was generally accepted that a husband had the right and duty to keep his wife in line – by force, if necessary. A poem written at the time sums up the role of the wife:

> 'She must kneel down at his bidding –
> From his feet his shoes unbind,
> Even if his whip descendeth
> On her head, she must not mind.'

The law supported this view. Before 1878 aggravated assault by a husband provided no grounds for a separation by the courts and, even after that date, it was often regarded as 'permissable, just chastisement'.

SILLIEST PROTEST

In order to stop a road being built through a forest in Queensland, an Australian conservationist Mr John Groothedde tied his testicles to a two-ton block of concrete. He was arrested and freed with the help of the local fire brigade.

MOST REVEALING INSIGHT INTO THE SEX LIFE OF LIBRARIANS

One of London's leading reference libraries contains the following instruction in its central index: 'SEX, See MENTAL CONFLICT'.

TOUGHEST MARITAL CONTRACT

A German court has been told recently of the case of Hans and Elsa Mayer, a couple who had been married for twenty-four years.

Hans told the court that, on their wedding night, Elsa had surprised him by imposing three conditions 'before anything happened'. They were:

1. That Hans should give Elsa the entire wage packet, unopened, every week.

2. That he should pay her £5 out of what she returned to him, every time they made love.

3. That he should never mention his occupation of gravedigger since it upset her.

After the birth of their second child, the rate under Item 2, Hans explained, was raised to £10. 'It was very difficult for me,' he said. 'I couldn't save enough out of my spending money to pay her. I asked for credit but she refused to give me any. In nineteen years, I could only afford to have her fifteen times.'

Before sentencing Hans to seven months' gaol for the rape of Elsa's cousin, the judge asked him why he married a wife who imposed such harsh conditions on him.

'Before we married everything was free,' he replied mournfully.

His wife confirmed the truth of his story. 'Nothing in life is free,' she said.

MOST UNNERVING QUESTION FROM THE BENCH

The eminent peer Lord Wigoder likes to remind those about to enter the legal profession of the importance of using precisely the right words in public by telling the story of one of the first cases he tried.

A surly youth, who was chewing a toffee, appeared in the dock before him. 'I frowned at him and asked him if he was masticating,' Wigoder recalls. 'The witness quickly took his hands from his pockets.'

MOST SEXUALLY INACTIVE TOWN IN BRITAIN

An April Fool joke has cast an unflattering light on the sex life of the citizens of Braintree, Essex. Mr Jim Dawson called on more than forty households on a local council estate, armed with a clipboard and a faked official letter on the morning of 1 April, and told them that, as from that month, a local rate supplement would be raised on any couple who had committed sexual intercourse that week on council property. The sum was 50p per act and was payable automatically if one or both partners 'reached completion'.

'It was a flop, I'm afraid,' Mr Dawson told the local paper. 'I was hoping to raise some money for charity and get a bit of a laugh as well. But no one thought it was in the least surprising and only one couple gave me 50p. One woman asked me if the new tax was retrospective to last year. Another said I should get about fifteen quid from her neighbours, but the neighbours turned out to be a family of wrestlers.'

MOST PARANOID WIFE

'Dear Abby

I've been married two years and my wife is tops. In my profession I deal with women who are sort of "on the loose", and at times I walk into a kiss. I explain this to my wife, but she doesn't seem to understand. If I chance to get kissed, I wipe the lipstick off with my handkerchief and throw it away, but now she counts my handkerchiefs and lets me know when one is missing. How can I get my wife to trust me again?

"Not Trusted" '

MOST CAREFULLY ORGANIZED MILITARY EXERCISE

Friends of twenty-three-year-old army boxing champion Lt Corporal Rainer Kern were astonished by a drunken confession he made to them one night, a West

German military court was told. Despite being tall, muscular and attractive, Kern was still a virgin.

Determined to solve this problem, Kern's friend and room-mate Corporal Bernhard Sighi smuggled a girl into their barracks in the back of an army truck.

But even with the girl waiting for him in his bed, Kern had an attack of nerves and refused to come out of his corner for the first round, until Sighi took over.

Bernhard then clicked his heels and shouted 'Lieutenant Corporal, drop trousers and prepare to face the enemy!' Kern told the court, 'First I refused, but then he pulled rank and showed me how it was done.'

The next morning, all three were found in the same bed an hour after reveille by an officer.

Both men were sentenced to two weeks solitary confinement in the glasshouse for breach of discipline and moral turpitude.

LEAST PERVERTED FEMININE WOMAN

Voted 'Feminine Woman of the Year' in 1984 by the nationwide Campaign for the Feminine Woman, Mrs Annie Wilton-Jones told the press some of the secrets of her success. She never allowed herself to watch television or listen to the radio for fear of being contaminated by 'the perverted indoctrination of the Women's Libbers', and she never disagreed with her husband.

One day when she scraped the family car, Mrs Wilton-Jones was so ashamed that she suggested to her husband that he 'dealt with her later'. The Feminine Woman of the Year told journalists. 'The knowledge that the matter could be dealt with so as to assuage my guilt and relieve his annoyance by a short spanking allowed us both to relax.'

FREEST CHURCH OUTING

A Free Church coach tour of the Lake District began to go seriously wrong when Miss Maureen Welter, a secretary, insisted on bathing in her underclothes in Derwentwater, a magistrates court was later told.

'Our minister warned her this could incite the coach driver,' said Thomas Gain, who was in the dock, 'and at least three of her fellow tourists asked her not to jump up and down in front of them while shouting "Spring time! Spring time!" '

Gain's prediction about the coach driver proved to be correct. The man moved the coach off but, instead of driving to Helvellyn Heights where the group was supposed to have tea, he took it down a secluded lane. There he stopped, got out with Miss Welter, and, a few moments later, started making love on a bank.

'Most people chose to ignore them,' said Gain, 'but when they went at it for the third time I saw red.' He had then allegedly approached the couple at a run and bitten Miss Welter so hard on the buttocks that she was in pain for several days and would be 'permanently scarred'.

'I was anxious for my tea,' the defendant explained. 'The intolerable delay drove me to a frenzy.'

SOPPIEST HIPPY

A lonely heart from the personal columns of *Event*:

KEVIN (22) would like a girlfriend to sit in a field, full of buttercups, and hold hands with him. Box F235.

ODDEST PAPAL INCIDENT

Listening to the Pope speak from the balcony in St Peter's Square on the dangers of casual sex, a tourist in the crowd, Miss Nancy Miller, had an unpleasant experience. 'I felt a hand lift my skirt,' she said, 'and shortly afterwards a man began to make love to me. I didn't like to call attention to what was going on because of the occasion. But as soon as the Pope had finished, I turned round and slapped the face of the man who was standing behind me. Unfortunately for us both he turned out to be a Miss Elstrom from Copenhagen, who was wearing her husband's clothes because it was a very cold day.'

SEVEN

TOO ROMANTIC

'There's no such thing as romantic love. Every normally constituted young man wants to pop into bed with every normally constituted young woman. And vice versa. That's all there is to it.'

H. G. Wells

UNHAPPIEST ANIMAL-LOVER

Sentenced to be hung after having been found guilty in 1662 of many 'damnable bestialities' with different types of domestic animals, a sixty-year-old farm labourer from New Haven was preceded on to the gallows by a cow, two heifers, three sheep, and two sows. The man was reported to be in tears as he saw his loved ones being executed before him.

DOTTIEST ROMANTIC GESTURE

Over fifty drivers stopped to offer Mr Orlando William a lift as he crawled on his hands and knees beside a road near Youngsville, Florida. He refused, explaining that he was on his way to the house of Miss Robin Seebez, a woman with whom he had fallen in love six days previously.

When he arrived, with torn trousers and bloodied palms, at Miss Seebez's house, she told him he was the stupidest person she had ever met and tried to strangle him with a skipping rope.

Speaking later from a hospital bed, William said, 'She is the only one for me.'

LEAST CONSISTENT PROHIBITIONIST

A veteran marriage-hater, H. L. Mencken, was once told by a friend that marriage was once a wonderful institution. 'Yes,' he replied, 'but who would want to live in an institution?'

He told his friend and biographer Charles Angoff that even his sexual needs were of a minor order. 'When you begin to push fifty, you really don't need to get yourself wet in the central heating as often as before. Sometimes a whole week goes by now and sexually I'm a Prohibitionist.'

Then, at the age of forty-nine, he astonished the American literary scene by getting married to Sara Haardt, whom he had met at one of his lectures.

'It is a grand experience to be able to look a hotel detective in the eye,' he explained.

LEAST DIGNIFIED TRAGIC GESTURE

After a love affair had gone wrong, a man in Lagny, France, tried to gas himself but, while lighting a last cigarette, caused an explosion. Finding that he was on fire, the man jumped into a water tank and drowned.

MOST POMPOUS REFERENCE TO THE PERMISSIVE SOCIETY IN THE 'MAIL ON SUNDAY'

'In 1964, a survey showed that only one in eight English girls had lost their virginity by the time they left their teens. By 1980, a new survey showed that five out of six girls had done so. This was the result of what became known as the permissive society. Whether anybody is more happier (sic) or more fulfilled at the virtual extinction of the English Rose is a matter of debate.'

LEAST HISTORICALLY RELEVANT FACT ABOUT THE LIFE OF GOETHE

It is now known that Christine, the wife of the great German writer Goethe, referred to his penis as 'Herr Schonfuss', or 'Mr Nice-Foot'.

MOST POETIC EXPRESSION OF SOD'S LORE

In Sir Richard Burton's translation of *The Book of the Thousand and One Nights*, there is told the story of Queen Budur who was separated from her husband Kamarin-al-Zaman by war. To protect herself, the queen dressed as a man as she searched for her husband throughout the land. When she eventually found him, she was afraid to reveal her disguise but

wanted to take him to bed. The king was reluctant but the stranger argued that the act was entirely natural:

> 'The penis smooth and round
> Was made with anus to match it;
> Had it been made for cunnus' sake
> It had been formed like a hatchet.'

The king was so impressed with this logic that he agreed and they retired to bed where, after noticing that she 'did not have a tool like the tools of men', he quickly realized who the stranger was.

FRIENDLIEST GESTURE IN CRICKET HISTORY

From the *Daily Telegraph* in 1949:

> 'Compton repeatedly strode down the pitch and reached out for Stollmeyer's goolies.'

STRANGEST SULTAN

Moulay Ismael, the Sultan of Morocco, was celebrated in his own time for a particular party trick. When mounting his horse, he would leap into the saddle, sword in hand, simultaneously decapitating the slave who was holding his stirrup. During his reign, 30,000 slaves were said to have died this way.

The Sultan was scarcely more endearing in his romantic life. He used to send choice specimens of his bowel movements to ladies of the court as a mark of special favour.

MOST REASONABLE REQUEST

Asked by a local official why she wanted to change her christian name to 'Esther', a Virginian student Miss Easy Blow explained that her name had caused misunderstandings and embarrassment.

SIMPLEST ASTROLOGICAL ADVICE

According to astrological love in sixth century Mesopotamia, the best lovers are born under the following signs:

Men for women – Libra
Women for men – Pisces
Men for men – Scorpio

The most encouraging sign for 'women for women' encounters was not mentioned.

MOST CONFUSED SCHOOLGIRL

Disappointed that her school would not be inviting her to the annual school dinner because she had posed nude for *Men Only* while still a pupil, seventeen-year-old Debee Ashby told the *Daily Star*, 'It's a disappointment – I wanted to show that the pictures caused no hard feelings.'

SHORTEST-LIVED LOVE SITUATION

An item from the agony column in the *Belfast Sunday News* aptly sums up the experience of many young girls:

'Dear Abby
    My boyfriend (21) and I (19) have a very beautiful love relationship but he says he doesn't "like" me. He says he "loves" me, but that is only when we are in a love situation.'

MOST ONE-HANDED SEXUAL LIBERATION

'The reason I like Jim,' wrote one Suzy Hickford about ageing hippy Jim Haynes, 'is because he comes while he masturbates me and I don't even have to touch him. And then afterwards he says that it was like his third ever orgasm when he was about thirteen. He's an old man now.

'In these troubled times many writers have come to light but Jim isn't one of them. Seriously though, he thinks the answer to everything is masturbation. He's wrong; the answer to most things is fucking. Actually Jim's all right and I didn't mean what I said about his writing.'

Haynes was so touched by this zonked-out testimonial that he included it in his autobiography, the embarrassingly entitled *Thanks for Coming!*

BEST NEWS FOR SEXLESS, TALKATIVE, DANCING GLUTTONS

Proving that the United Nations does in fact have a world role, the results of 1971 UN survey into the state of marriage suggested that too much sex could ruin a marriage. Those trapped in dangerous 'sex-based' marriages should seek substitutes for this harmful activity. The report particularly recommended dancing, eating out and good conversation.

SILLIEST BARMAN

Appearing before the local magistrate on a charge of assault and battery, Mr George Thomas, a bartender at the Chocolate Poodle in Nantwich explained that the victim of the attack, Miss Elsie Queen, had provoked him unnecessarily.

'Elsie and I had spent the evening looking at each other. Her friend explained that she was deaf and dumb. I was very keen on her and managed to arrange a date for the next day – though it took the best part of an hour to do so.

'Two days later, when she hadn't turned up, I popped into the Star and saw her standing on a chair singing "You Are My Sunshine" loud and clear. Then I saw red and punched her.'

SADDEST GRAND FINALE

Despairing that his love for a local flautist would ever be requited, Monsieur Philomel Crasny from Vincennes committed suicide by causing a carefully balanced grand piano to fall on his head.

FRIENDLIEST SANTA

A heavily promoted Christmas grotto, complete with its own Santa, provided a pet shop in Liskeard, Cornwall, with more publicity than it was bargaining for when a local reporter spotted a queue of over-excited secretaries and shop workers waiting for their turn outside the shop.

Intrigued as to why no children were in the queue, the reporter investigated and discovered the special yuletide attraction was Chris Christmas, the aptly named local man who was playing the part of Santa. 52-year-old Chris was eagerly providing kisses and cuddles in the grotto for the town's frustrated women-folk.

Speaking later to the *Sun*, whose story FATHER KISSMAS IN RED-HOT GROTTO SCANDAL gave the incident national prominence, Chris's wife Mrs Margaret Christmas said she was fuming. 'I couldn't believe it when I saw a queue of women without children waiting to sit on his knee. His beard was all covered in lipstick,' she said.

Father Kissmas was unabashed. 'I don't discourage the girls,' he said, 'I've cuddled nearly a hundred in here.'

His wife was later reported to be guarding the red-hot grotto with a rolling pin.

EIGHT

TOO CONFUSED

'Fortunately for me, at the time when sex was beginning to loom in my life as an enormous and insoluble problem, I began to take an interest in keeping animals.'

Armand Denis

MOST ORIGINAL MEDICAL ADVICE FROM THE WEST COAST

It is now sensible for women to have their breasts removed well before any cancer is detected to avoid it spreading to other parts of the body, according to an article in the *New York Times* by Dr Penis, a plastic surgeon from San Francisco.

MOST CONFUSED EROTICIST

For one who was later to bring relief to millions of lonely people with such classics of erotica as *Delta of Venus* and *Little Birds*, Anais Nin was oddly innocent as a young girl about the way men are made. 'She had thought,' wrote Edmund Wilson in *The Twenties*, 'that men's cocks were stiff all the time because whenever they got close enough to notice, they always were – when men danced with her and when she was a little girl and when they'd hold her on their legs – the dirty things!'

MOST PERCEPTIVE CRIMINAL CHARGE

A report from the lawcourts section of the *Yorkshire Post* of August 1984:

> 'A man found in a car with his trousers down and a woman astride him was arrested for impersonating a police officer, Leeds magistrates were told yesterday.'

LEAST PUBLICIZED SOVIET INVENTION

Concerned at the country's falling birth rate, Russian doctors have come up with a new and original incentive. A woman's sexual pleasure, according to the official reports which are widely publicised, occurs most intensely after the birth of the first child.

Contrary to what is believed in the West, the Central Committee is aware of the intimate problems of family life. In 1972, it accepted an invention patented by the Committee of Inventions of the Council of Ministers, and described as 'a device designed to intensify women's sexual excitement'.

Despite many enquiries from Western Europe and America, the invention has not yet been available for export.

MOST DISAPPOINTED KNEE-TREMBLER

Accused during the late sixteenth century of having 'got Margaret Moneley with child', farmer John Cotgreve was outraged. He told the court: 'Cockes wounds! Can a man get a child standing? For I never had anything to do with her but standing!'

MOST UNUSUAL INSIGHT INTO BRITISH POST-COITAL BEHAVIOUR

According to his biographer Michael Howard, the publisher Jonathan Cape liked to place his own personal stamp on the manuscripts he edited. When he found the passage in Simone de Beauvoir's *The Second Sex* describing the pleasure of a post-coital cigarette, he firmly crossed out 'cigarette' and substituted 'pipe'.

MOST SEXIST SEXOLOGIST

A glimpse into the secret life of the frustrated executive wife was provided by a talk to a group of expatriate Americans living in Brussels by sex expert Robert Whitney, who had flown in from the States specially for the occasion.

For some reason, the wives were unimpressed when he told them encouragingly that the job they did around the home was *just* as important, in its way, as that which their husbands did.

117

'Then why the hell don't we get paid for it?' shouted one wife.

The meeting grew unruly when Whitney suggested that staying late at the office was to be tolerated by wives of high-flying executives. Several wives disagreed, yelling that they should get themselves good lovers.

'To further hubby's chances of promotion,' Whitney continued, 'it is important to have periodic talks and scheduled discussion times. You all know the best times you can talk to your guys —'

'Before sex!' shouted one wife.

'What sex?' yelled another.

Moments later, the sexologist was escorted out of the meeting in a state of shock and confusion.

SILVER MEDAL FOR BUREAUCRATIC THOROUGHNESS

After West German authorities had announced that a ten foot wall would separate men and women competitors at the Olympic Village for the Munich Games, a reporter humorously asked whether the wall was expected to keep out pole-vaulters. The vaulters would be asked to check in their poles at the gate, the man was told.

LEAST ENTHUSIASTIC FIANCEE

'Dear Abby

Last year I had an affair with a girl seven inches taller and three years older than myself. She wanted to get married but I promised my mother I'd never marry a girl out of my own faith. Then, too, I have a heart murmur and I don't think it would be fair to the girl. Also I can't afford it. Then there's the problem of our differing sizes and ages. Don't you think these are legitimate reasons for staying single?
"Seeking Advice" '

MOST OUTRAGEOUS CASE OF SEXUAL DISCRIMINATION

According to the New York weekly *Village Voice*, the city's first masturbation workshop is doing brisk business.

'We specialize in breathing techniques and advanced pelvic movements,' the workshop's manager Betty Dodson explained. 'It's all about getting into real sexual energy.'

After receiving hundreds of enquiries from potential masturbators in the New York area, Miss Dodson found she had to limit classes. Her first step was to rule out the possibility of men joining the classes.

'After an in-depth study, I found that masturbation lessons for men just did not exist,' she said.

STRANGEST STATISTIC

In 1984, a MORI poll was commissioned to discover which was the sexiest party in Britain today. The results provided a bizarre insight into the private life of political activists. Women members of each party were asked: 'Have you ever had sex with anybody beside your present partner?' The following percentages said 'yes':

> Alliance – 33%
> Conservative – 33%
> Labour – 26%

While most commentators suggested that this was a major defeat for Labour, the more perceptive of them spotted another fascinating statistic. In answer to the above question, no less than 1% of all Conservative women replied 'Don't know'.

MOST EXPENSIVE ORGASM

Believing that a man's sperm is directly connected to his cerebral matter and that therefore every emission involved the waste of creative powers, Honoré de Balzac was a compulsive self-interrupter. As the Goncourts described in their diary, 'He was perfectly happy playing the love game up to the point of ejaculation, but he was unwilling to go further.'

Unfortunately, one night in a Paris brothel, the novelist lost his usual self-control and, in spite of himself, took 'the love game' to its full, satisfying conclusion. The next day he was devastated. 'I lost a novel this morning!' he wailed.

MELLOWEST SEX CLUB

At the Xanadu's Perfumed Garden sex club in San Francisco, the management have organized some very West Coast attractions. There's an SM fantasy workshop on Wednesday nights as well as parties for women only 'to help them enjoy public nudity', Aqua-Energetics or pool therapy and a workshop where married couples 'learn to forgive each other'.

A word of warning to male members of the Xanadu. Its owner Luisa Castro, who has a master's degree in Human Sexuality, firmly discourages men from 'handling women as objects without recognizing their sensitivities.'

Whether women receive the same stern warning is not clear.

MOST EASILY CURED NEUROTIC

A married woman from Leatherhead described by her psychiatrist as being 'a compulsive handwasher with a morbid fear of difficulties', was helped through her difficulties by bribes of Polo mints, for which she had a craving. Her handwashing was soon completely cured and she was advised to keep packets of the mint with a hole around the house to help her establish normal sexual relations with her husband.

MOST BORING FANTASY

Daily Mail columnist Lynda Lee-Potter came up with a surprising confession in February 1985. Commenting on a report that showed that most women have regular romantic and sexual fantasies, she revealed the true dullness of her own imaginative self. 'My only fantasy,' she wrote proudly, 'is silence, solitude and total inertia.'

MOST PRURIENT POLICE FORCE

After a group of eight-year-olds, encouraged by their schoolmistress, built a snow woman to accompany a snowman that had been built the day before, local police requested the school authorities to remove its breasts. Neighbours might complain, they pointed out.

MOST TEASED TRANSVESTITE

Short, dumpy and effete, the Chevalier d'Eon de Beaumont was something of a joke in the early eighteenth century at the court of St James where he served as a low-order diplomat (and part-time spy) on behalf of the French government. When the French ambassador himself was heard to denounce d'Eon as a hermaphrodite, speculation was rife at the court and

significant bets were placed. Was the Chevalier man, woman or a bit of both?

Afraid of being kidnapped and stripped in order to resolve the bets, d'Eon appealed to the French king, whose reply was less than helpful. As a good Frenchman, said the king, d'Eon could not be seen to discredit the French ambassador to London. He could therefore return to France and safety, but only on one condition. He would have to admit that he was a woman and live his life dressed accordingly.

D'Eon, who had a state pension to think of, agreed. He went into hibernation in order to get used to his new persona and his new dresses which, to judge from his correspondence of the time, was not easy.

'I am as foolish as a fox who has lost his tail,' he wrote. 'I am trying to walk in pointed shoes with high heels, but have nearly broken my neck more than once; it has happened that, instead of making a courtesy, I have removed my wig and three-tiered head-dress, taking them for my hat or helmet.'

When he arrived in Paris, d'Eon was a sensation – but like all fashions, was quickly forgotten. He tired of dressing in women's clothing and returned to England to die poor – but with his sex no longer in doubt.

MOST OBVIOUS CASE OF SHARED GUILT

A Hollywood divorce court in the 1950s was told how the marriage of a film executive and his wife had broken down. One night, they were asleep together and the wife had a vivid dream that she was making love to her lover when her husband walked in. 'My husband! My husband!' she shouted in her sleep.

Hearing the shrieks, her husband leapt out of bed and hid in the wardrobe.

SEXISTS' FAVOURITE SAINT

'The woman is subject to the man on account of the weakness of her nature, both of mind and of body . . . Man is the beginning of woman and her end, just as God is the beginning and end of every creature, woman is in subjection according to the law of nature, but a slave is not.'

St Thomas Aquinas (1225–1274)

SEXISTS' FAVOURITE RELIGIOUS TEXT

'The source of dishonour is woman; the source of strife is woman; the source of earthly existence is woman; therefore avoid woman.'

The Code of Manu, a religious text from ancient India.

SEXISTS' FAVOURITE RELIGIOUS LEADER

'Take women from their housewifery and they are good for nothing . . . If women get tired and die of bearing, there is no harm in that; let them die as long as they bear; they are made for that.'

Martin Luther (1483–1546)

SEXISTS' FAVOURITE LEGAL SYSTEM

'One of the most painful and horrible things that one comes across in these days are the dreadful traits one finds in the female,' said Mr Justice Humphreys in 1936 while summing up a case in which a boy of sixteen stood accused of having sex with a girl of thirteen. The judge went on to regret that he was not legally allowed to gaol the girl as well as the boy for this heinous crime.

Two years earlier Mr Justice Charles had told *The Times* that 'as he and his brother judges went round the country they found there were a very large number of young men, boys really, who were charged with offences with girls under the age of sixteen. In his experience, he found that the fault very often lay with the girl.'

In March 1933, an eighteen-year-old girl from Stoke-on-Trent was tried for the murder of an illegitimate child that had been born after a brief liaison with a married man when the girl was sixteen. The jury found her 'guilty with a strong recommendation to mercy'.

The judge, Mr Justice Horridge, sentenced her to death.

LEAST ENDOWED FLASHER

Passers-by were more intrigued than shocked when a man in a heavy fur coat started flashing on Clapham High Street. Even those who looked away as quickly as possible couldn't fail to notice that this flasher was not entirely as other flashers are. In fact, he appeared to have nothing to flash.

At a South London court, Edwin Johnson, alias Linda Gold, explained that he had recently had a sex-change operation and was so pleased with it that he wanted to show it off in public. The police officer filling in the charge sheet had placed a question mark under the heading 'Sex'.

MOST DISASTROUS ADOLESCENT MISUNDERSTANDING

In his autobiography *A Bishop's Confession*, the American writer Jim Bishop tells the cautionary tale of his sexual initiation. After months of adolescent fantasies about a local girl he calls Tessie, he was invited up to her house when her parents were out. Having agreed to go, he was gripped by panic. 'What could I do with a grown woman, seventeen-years-old? The fellows on the corner said you spread her legs and put your thing in her thing: But what was her thing like?'

When he arrived at the house, Tessie called to him from the bedroom. He found her lying on the bed in a swimsuit with her eyes closed. Courageously – and with some difficulty – he removed the swimsuit. Tessie never stirred.

As she lay there naked in the dark, Jim became worried as to where exactly 'her thing' was. 'There was but one way to make certain. I reached into my sagging trouser pockets and pulled out a kitchen match. I struck it on my shoe and, when the flame flared, I held it high up between Tessie's thighs to ascertain the what and the where. For no reason whatever, the girl popped straight up in the air screaming. Then she held her hand over her mouth. She stood nude in the dark whispering: "Get out, you little son of a bitch! Get out, you goddam pervert!" '

Trousers at half-mast, Jim fled.

BEST ATTEMPT TO RUIN 'MINDER'

Writing in the *British Journal of Family Planning*, Dr David Delvin has criticized the scriptwriters on the TV series *Minder* for ignoring the problem of unwanted pregnancies.

'When did you last see Terry take a contraceptive out of his pocket before leaping between the sheets with this week's lovely?' asks the doctor. 'I wish he could be heard to say on the screen, "Are you on the pill or shall I use a sheath?" '

MOST CONFUSING INSTRUCTION FROM GERMAINE GREER

'The first thing on earth to be sold was cunt. And it will be the last,' Germaine Greer, former groupie and born-again guru of sexual restraint told *Time Out*. 'It's the paradigm of all selling. I don't know if we've a hope in hell of overturning that. But I'm determined to try and I'll use any technique of saying "yes" or technique of saying "no" or a technique of saying "suck my foot for the next three weeks and then ... maybe".'

LEAST APPRECIATED GENIUS

'You can't leave it to Aldous,' said Maria Huxley about her determinedly unfaithful husband, 'he'd make a muddle.'

It was possibly the confidence that Aldous would make a muddle that allowed Maria to give her husband a free rein in his extramarital affairs, which normally ended disastrously.

One of his lovers, Dora Carrington, wrote vividly to Lytton Strachey about a night spent with the famous author of *Brave New World* when they were both guests of Lady Ottoline Morrell.

'Such a nightmare last night with Aldous in bed, everything went wrong. I could not lock the door: all the bolts were crooked. At last I chained it with a watch chain on the nails. Then I had a new pair of thick pyjamas on and he got cross because I wouldn't take them off and they were all scratchy. Everything got in a mess, and he got angry, and kept on trying to find me in bed by peering with his eye-glass, and I thought all the time how I could account to my mother for the mess on my pyjamas.'

Later in his life, Huxley pursued Nancy Cunard with scarcely more success. Going to bed with Aldous, Cunard once confided to a friend, was 'like being crawled over by slugs'.

NINE

TOO PUBLIC

'Never fornicate through an ink
bottle.'

Dion Boucicault

LEAST DIPLOMATIC CONGRESSMAN

There was a minor political storm in 1971 in America when Congressman Wilbur Mills was asked at a public meeting what he planned to do about winning civil rights for the twenty million gays currently living in the country. 'Twenty *million!*' Mills was heard to mutter, 'Shit, I'm getting out of here.'

HIGHEST LOVE DUEL

Having fallen out over the affections of a lady, Monsieur de Grandpré and Monsieur Le Piquet decided in 1808 to fight an unusual duel. Each of them would be armed with a blunderbuss and would fight from identically sized and designed balloons over Paris. Le Piquet missed with his first shot and when his opponent scored a direct puncture, plunged to his death in the Jardin des Tuileries.

MOST MISUNDERSTOOD FLAUTIST

'It took several years of hard training to bring the act to perfection. I have performed throughout the U.S. Several mayors have praised my work.'

Miss Hula Biggles was explaining why she had decided to sue the Detroit state authorities for banning her act and condemning it as 'lewd and tasteless'. She claimed that very few artistes were able to play the flute through the vagina in the way that she did.

'I concentrate on patriotic songs,' said Miss Biggles, 'and I also sing the words to the tune.'

BUTCHEST QUEEN

The formidable Queen Christina of Sweden was so determinedly masculine in her appearance, dress and behaviour that she was believed by many of her subjects to be a hermaphrodite. In order to set the record straight, the queen arranged for her carriage to be overturned one day. As she lay on the ground in a state of disorder, she was seen to heave her clothes up around her waist. 'Come closer,' she ordered her attendants, 'come and convince yourselves that I'm no hermaphrodite.'

Years later, Queen Christina abdicated and left Sweden dressed in men's clothing, and calling herself 'Count Dohna'.

LEAST CLASSY SUPERSTUD

Describing the life-style of a gigolo to the *Sun*, Michael Hizer described how he has designed his flat for sex. 'I've got all the gear,' he boasted, 'a suede bed with stereo in the headboard, and a cocktail cabinet in arm's

reach. There's a gold plaque on the door saying "The Stud Farm" so they know what they're in for.'

HEAVIEST STAGE PERFORMANCE

Arrested in 1981 for 'pandering obscenity', Wendy O. Williams, whose group The Plasmatics were extreme practitioners of what they called 'Pornography Rock', said, 'I'm a rock 'n' roll singer – I should be able to do what I want.'

Given the nature of their act, it was hardly surprising that the police should take an interest in The Plasmatics. In his book *Rock 'n' Roll Babylon*, Gary Herman describes what he called 'the ultimate sex-and-violence act to date'.

'Sporting a Mohican haircut, Wendy might come on in a see-through body-stocking, or tight black pants and some strategically placed sticky tape – sometimes she would opt for no more than a couple of blobs of whipped cream to cover her nipples. The all-male Plasmatics looked no less bizarre and the music – if that's the right word – fitted the image. Songs like *Sex Junkie*, *Pig is a Pig* and *Living Dead* were hammered out with all the subtlety of an exploding elephant. Guitarist Richie Scott whacked himself over the head with his guitar. Wendy smashed televisions, took a chain-saw to a plugged-in guitar and sliced it in two, and at the climax of the act, the group might demolish an entire motor car.'

The incident in 1981 was not the first run-in Wendy and the boys had had with the pigs. The previous year in Milwaukee, she had been dragged out of the concert hall, screaming and kicking.

'One of them grabbed my tits, another grabbed my rear end – so I smacked them,' the singer explained later. 'I'd have gone along peacefully but I was outraged intellectually.'

GAMEST GRANDMUM

When Danish police raided a strip club in 1966, they arrested, among others, the club's main attraction – 'Tuppy', a sixty-six-year-old stripping grandmother.

'I strip to supplement my pension,' she said.

MOST CONTROVERSIAL TESTICLES

There was uproar in the village of Bentham when a statue of a Minotaur was put up outside the parish church.

'We were allowed to think that it would be an abstract piece that would give offence to nobody,' said Miss Gillian Percy, a local florist. 'But when the Minotaur appeared it was like a bombshell.'

Henry Conham, a retired market gardener from Bentham, was more direct. 'What is the point of going to church if the first thing you see when you come out is a pair of bollocks, each one bigger than a marrow?' he asked.

The rural council agreed to consider the removal of all or part of the statue.

MOST LIFTED FAMOUS FACE

The actress Merle Oberon was so concerned that she should remain attractive for as long as possible that she visited a plastic surgeon on a regular basis. Finally she had had so many facelifts that she was obliged to sleep with her eyes open.

LIGHTEST LET-OFF FOR CAMEL-DRIVERS AND SAILORS

During the Talmudic period of Judaism, religious writers established a minimum of marital rights that could be expected by wives. It was decreed that husbands should make love to their wives regularly – depending on the husband's occupation:

Gentlemen of leisure – every night
Labourers – twice weekly
Donkey drivers – once a week
Scholars – once a week (normally on Friday night)
Camel-drivers – once every thirty days
Sailors – once every six months

MOST FREQUENTLY INSULTED STARLET

There's something about actress and model Maria Harper that brings out the beast in famous superstuds, according to an interview with her published in the *Sun*.

Stud No. 1: Ryan O'Neal
'There was no pleasant introduction or polite small talk,' says Maria, recalling her only meeting with him. 'His only verbal foreplay was, "Take your clothes off, and come and test the jacuzzi with me." '

When politely rejected, O'Neal snapped, 'Suit yourself – it's your loss. You'll never have anyone as good as me.'

Stud No. 2: Warren Beatty
Warren Beatty's attempt to get to know the popular starlet was even more pathetic. At the reception for *Reds*, he ogled her from across the room and then sent over a drink with his compliments – a somewhat meaningless gesture since the drinks were free, says Maria. 'It began to get ridiculous when he sent someone over to let me know that he found me very attractive. Why couldn't the world's greatest lover tell me himself?'

Stud No. 3: Lewis Collins
But, compared to the behaviour of Lewis Collins of *The Professionals*, O'Neal and Beatty had showed old world charm. 'Get her over to the pub and get some drinks down her,' he said pointing Maria out to the film crew during a lunch-break. Down at the pub, he leant over to her and said, 'Fancy a quickie?'

Despite this unpromising beginning, Maria and Collins became lovers. 'Deep down he is a very sensitive person and not very confident about his sexual prowess,' Maria recalled. 'Lewis always insisted on making love with the lights out and I never got to see him naked at all.'

141

LOWEST BUDGET SKIN PICS

A couple from Portsmouth had known each other for fifteen minutes before they were seen entering a photo booth together at Portsmouth Central station. They were later arrested trying to sell obscene pictures of themselves committing a sex act to commuters on Platform 2.

The girl later told the court that she needed the money for a ticket to Haslemere to see her boyfriend.

MOST PATHETIC DISC JOCKEY

'I've turned to hunting girls in winebars and discos,' claims the self-proclaimed superstud of the airwaves Tony Blackburn in his autobiography *The Living Legend*. 'But I never press a girl to come to bed with me. I can tell when she's interested. I let her know I can't drive home because I've been drinking. Then I offer to call a cab or invite her home "because I'm expecting an important call". If she agrees to come back with me, it's not long before we're climbing the stairs to my king-sized bed.'

The swinging forty-two-year-old, who has told the world that he has made love to almost 250 girls, was briefly married to actress Tessa Wyatt. 'I wanted to possess her body and soul and it was all too much for her,' explains Tony.

MOST UNCONVENTIONAL CHORAL WORK

In Siberia, where the lumbermen see no women for months on end, a popular pastime is the so-called 'choir practice'. A prostitute is brought in and, while she makes public love to one man after another, the rest of the party sing patriotic songs and drink vodka.

MEANEST SOUL SINGER

When a Hollywood judge ordered the late Marvin Gaye to pay alimony and child support payments to Anna Gordy Gaye, to whom he had been married for fourteen years, by recording an album and handing over profits to the level of $600,000, the singer responded ungenerously. The album, entitled 'Here, My Dear', consisted largely of songs aimed at humiliating his former wife.

Anna had the last word however. The album was a massive flop and she used it to bring a five million dollar invasion of privacy suit against him.

SADDEST DAY FOR PARIS BROTHELS

Throughout his life Victor Hugo was almost as famous for his iron constitution and voracious sexual appetite as for his books. He claimed that he made love nine times on his wedding night and could happily take on three mistresses in one afternoon. Even his rival Saint-Beuve admitted that his physical vitality, even in his old age, was extraordinary. 'He's got an amazing constitution that man,' he wrote. 'His barber told me that his beard was three times as stiff as anybody else's and that it nicked all his razors.'

Well into his seventies, Hugo was a tireless frequenter of the best brothels of Paris – to such an extent that, on his death, the French government granted the prostitutes of Paris 70,000 francs so that they could join the mourners in the streets without losing money.

The Goncourt brothers recorded a particularly moving aspect of Hugo's funeral: 'Another detail about the *fucking* funeral rites for the great man – a detail which comes from the police. For the last week all the Fantines of the big brothels have carried on their trade with their natural parts draped in a scarf of black crepe – *their cunts in mourning.*'

THE WORLD'S FIFTH LEAST COMFORTABLE ROCK STAR IN HIS UNDERPANTS

Many observers of the pop world believe that the greatest asset a male rock n' roll singer possesses may not be his voice, his face, his songs, or even his manager, but what he's got down the front of his trousers.

Since the early days of rock, artists have been improving their intimate profiles with articles ranging in sophistication from a pair of woolly socks to a specially designed 12″ rayon thruster but, as trousers got tighter and the fans less easy to satisfy, the competition has become tougher at the bottom than ever before.

Ian Anderson of Jethro Tull tried to introduce a new element into his act by wearing a codpiece but the fashion never really caught on and eventually Anderson abandoned it himself, saying he was tired of 'waggling my codpiece and masturbating with my flute'.

THE WORLD'S FOURTH LEAST COMFORTABLE ROCK STAR IN HIS UNDERPANTS

Rod Stewart claims that nature has been kind and that the front of his trousers needs no artificial build-up. On the other hand, he does have a serious problem around the back. 'Rod wore very shiny, very tight pants onstage,' Britt Ekland has explained, 'and they were very tight around the bum. Because he wiggled it about so much on-stage, he wanted to keep it nice and smooth. But he couldn't have his instrument hanging all over the place, because it would dangle and it was very uncomfortable. So he used to take my knickers and pull them up real tight and stick the teeny weeny part up his bum.'

THE WORLD'S THIRD LEAST COMFORTABLE ROCK STAR IN HIS UNDERPANTS

So important a part of his act was Rod Stewart's bum-wiggling routine that, according to the magazine *Creem*, Barry Manilow engaged a Hollywood corsetier to work on a secret weapon – a pair of padded underpants to round out those groovy skin-tight flairs Barry wears on stage.

THE WORLD'S SECOND LEAST COMFORTABLE ROCK STAR IN HIS UNDERPANTS

The old-fashioned method of sticking things down the front of your trousers has distinct disadvantages, according to the singer Etta James.

Etta was standing backstage at a Rolling Stones concert in the mid-seventies, having opened for the group, when she noticed that Mick Jagger was having a certain amount of difficulty with what Etta calls 'that little package he wears in his pants'. During the familiar Jagger stage boogie, it had slipped down and was soon poking cheekily out of the bottom of his trousers. The consummate professional, Mick swaggered off, crouched down behind a speaker and hurriedly repositioned his little package while Keith Richard played an impromptu solo.

THE WORLD'S LEAST COMFORTABLE ROCK STAR IN HIS UNDERPANTS

Donny Osmond has the opposite problem. He prefers to wear special flattening pants and his management have been told to airbrush any hint of a frontal bulge out of publicity photographs.

MOST PRECARIOUS REVOLUTIONARY ACTIVITY

'Nude demonstrations' that would have done credit to California in the sixties used to take place frequently in Moscow following the Russian Revolution in 1917.

The Revolution had seen the end of all vestiges of bourgeois morality and, for a while, free love was regarded as an essential part of the revolution. In her essay *Make Way For Winged Eros*, Alexandra Kollontai wrote that sexual relationships should be conducted 'casually . . . in order to satisfy biological needs which both partners are eager to relieve so that they can concentrate their energies on what is essential: revolutionary activity.' Elsewhere, Kollontai compared making love to drinking a glass of water.

Suddenly, saying 'no' had become a revisionist aberration. 'Sexual abstinence is typical of the *petit bourgeois*,' wrote S. Sridovich in 1923. 'Every young Communist girl, whether a student in a worker's party or an ordinary student, upon whom any male has fixed his choice (I shall never understand how such African passions can have developed amongst us Nordics) ought to anticipate his desires; otherwise she is just a petite bourgeoise.'

Unfortunately the nude demonstrations, the most

open celebration of this revolutionary activity, were short-lived. For a while, naked men and women gathered in Petrograd and Moscow, held hands and sang, 'Love, love!' and 'Down with shame!' But then the Cheka, the political police, recruited groups of 'indignant workers' to harrass the demonstrators, many of whom were pursued, abused and goosed as they tried to make their way home naked.

It was the beginning of the end of the love revolution.

LEAST GENTLEMANLY OF CLUBS

During the eighteenth century, there was a vogue for secret clubs, which catered for Restoration versions of the Hooray Henry. According to Ned Ward's *The Secret History of London Clubs*, the most popular were:

> *The Mohocks*, who went out every night to stand women on their heads and look at their petticoats, roll people down the hill in barrels and generally beat them up.
> *The Sweaters*, who used to cut people with their swords.
> *The Bold Bucks*, whose speciality was rape.
> *The Blasters*, who enjoyed exposing themselves to passing women.
> *The Fun Club*, who played fatuous practical jokes on innocent bystanders.
> *The Hellfire Club*, who were famous for practising black magic and general promiscuity.
> *The Mollies*, who in Ward's words, 'try to speak, walk, chatter, shriek and scold as women do, aping them as well in other respects.'

MOST TOUCHING PATRIOTIC DISPLAY

Mr Adam Malik, Indonesian foreign minister, was both touched and disturbed by the greeting that awaited him when he visited the newly acquired province of Irian Jaya. One thousand local Dhani men were waiting at the airport wearing nothing more than 'kotekas', fifteen inch erect penis gourds, each one with an Indonesian flag on the tip.

After his departure, Mr Malik issued instructions that the Dhani men should, for the sake of decency, all be issued with shorts.

A few months later, the minister visited the province once more. The welcoming committee this time wore the shorts they had been issued – only the flies of each of them were undone and, poking through each pair were the same 'kotekas', flags waving proudly in the wind.

STRANGEST PUBLIC SPECTACLE

Mr Wallace Than of Hemsforth was so annoyed when his wife's lover failed to turn up at a pre-arranged meeting behind a public lavatory that he tore out four lavatory seats, draped them around Mrs Than's neck, and drove her around the town as a public spectacle.

MOST OUTRAGED SUCKER

'My action was never meant to be a piece of exhibitionism on my behalf,' wrote Germaine Greer to her ex-colleague Jim Haynes. 'It was meant to be a group action on the part of SUCK magazine.'

Greer was responding angrily to an incident that proved pivotal in the fortunes of SUCK, a sex magazine set up by ageing alternative gurus in the early 1970s. As one of the contributing editors, she had sent a number of nude photographs of herself to Haynes on the understanding that others involved in the magazine, including model Jean Shrimpton and playwright Heathcote Williams, would also pose nude for the magazine. They didn't and all that appeared was a full-page picture of Germaine peering at the camera through her legs, revealing a vast and intimate expanse of the Greer behind.

Since she was now a media celebrity, the photograph caused something of a frisson throughout the alternative society. 'The interesting point,' Haynes wrote later, trying to justify this totally uncool breach of confidence, 'is the women and readers of SUCK on the Continent, in France, Germany, Holland, wrote letters to the paper saying, "Right on, Germaine, we're behind you, this is great, good for you for doing it, it's absolutely appropriate . . ." I don't think Germaine got the positive feedback.'

In a letter to the editors of SUCK, Greer announced her resignation, dismissing the entire episode as 'just another example of the spuriousness of your pseudo-revolutionary aims.'

MOST UNSCHEDULED DEMONSTRATION AT A BARRATT HOME

An insurance salesman and his wife who had made a 9.30 appointment to visit a show house on the new Barratt's estate near Swansea were surprised to find a couple making love in the bedroom. A spokesman for Barratts revealed that the intruders had met at a local pub the previous night and that the girl had been reliably informed that the house belonged to her new boyfriend's mother.

LEAST LIKELY TEXTS FOR LATIN 'O' LEVEL

Graffiti found among remains of Pompeii have provided some valuable insights into the sex life of the average Roman. Erotic failures, it seems, were as much a part of life then as now. Some of the items on the walls of Pompeii were boastful:

'Hic ego nunc flutae formosa forma puella laudata a multis, set lutus intus erat.'
('Here I have now fucked a girl beautiful to see, praised by many, but there was much inside.')

Some were touching:

'Fonticulus pisciculo suo plurma salut.'
('Little Fountain says "Hello" to his little fishy.')

Some were businesslike:

'Lakis felat a.II.'
('Lakis blows for two pence.')

While some were simply odd:

'Miximus in lecto. Fateor, peccavimus, hospes si dices quare? Nulla matella fuit.'
('We have pissed in the bed. I admit, we were wrong, my host, if you ask me why? There was no chamber pot?')

TEN

TOO ENTHUSIASTIC

'Damn Nearly Everybody . . . If the boys didn't exist, I should have to invent them.'

Christopher Isherwood

SADDEST SPONSORED WALK

'Our eyes crossed while we were studying a methane contract issued by the Oregon Natural Gas Company,' said Mr Wayne Eyemouth of Peekie, Oregon, who was explaining why he had decided to set out on a sponsored Round-the-World-Love-March.

He had first attempted to win the hand of Miss Shelley Ziz by erecting a thirty foot high heart on the roof of his bungalow. When this had failed, Eyemouth had hit on the idea of walking around the world collecting signatures begging his beloved to change her mind.

It was after the first ten thousand signatures had arrived in Peekie that Miss Ziz took action. She married Wayne's younger brother Tyrone.

When the news reached him, the round-the-world-love walker was in a state of collapse in the intensive care unit of a Saudi Arabian hospital.

MOST CLAP-RIDDEN ITALIAN

During his lifetime, Casanova suffered from at least eleven attacks of venereal disease and, when he visited the town of Osera, he managed to infect over fifty people with gonorrhea.

The local doctor commented happily: 'For twenty years I have practised in this town where I lived in poverty . . . But ever since last year I can say that my condition has changed. I have made much money and invested it wisely.'

MOST UNUSUAL SIDE-EFFECT OF ALGEBRAIC EQUATIONS

There is no limit to the kind of thing that women in a certain frame of mind may find stimulating, as was proved by one of Havelock Ellis' more troubled patients.

'I have tried mechanical mental work such as solving arithmetical or algebraic problems, but it does no good,' she told him tremulously. 'In fact, it seems to increase the excitement.'

KEENEST PARTY ACTIVISTS

Explaining why they came to lodge a complaint with the local police, Daniel Bamford, one of a party entertainment duo, had a bizarre tale to tell.

'We call ourselves the Oddballs,' he said, 'and as we have performed our dance – naked except for socks and cleverly placed balloons – all over the South of England for many years, it came as no surprise when we were invited to appear at a party given by the women members of the Wimbledon Conservative Club. However, just as we were getting into the songs, the ladies became terribly excited and rushed us with pins and lighted cigarettes in their hands. Over 150 balloons were popped and my partner Richard Welsh had his wedding tackle bruised.'

MOST TYPICAL JOURNALISTIC ACHIEVEMENT

After an Italian gigolo had claimed, amidst much publicity, that he had made love to 18,000 women, a *Daily Mirror* reporter, who preferred to remain anonymous, claimed his own record – he had been *rejected* 18,000 times.

Among the turn-downs he was in a fit state to remember were:

We might start the dog barking.
My husband will be back in half an hour.
The usherette might see us.
I like you too much.
I don't like you enough.
Ask my friend – I'm tired.
No.
No, thank you.
It's manners to wait until you are asked.
I made myself this promise two years ago and I mean
    to keep it.
I don't think my boyfriend would approve.
I'm under the doctor at the moment.
It would spoil a beautiful relationship.
What! After church?
I never go with journalists.
That sort of thing's for animals.
We'd break the deckchair.
Not in the sand.
We might drown.
My sunburn hurts too much.
The walls are paper thin.
I never do it on the first night.
The moment has been and gone now.
I'm a lesbian.
You look as if you might have herpes.
I'd rather wait until we're married.
I'm going to forget you ever said that.

All I want right now, thank you, is a nice cup of tea.
I feel far too maternal towards you.
Be a good boy and put it away.
I suppose you're a reporter looking for a story.
Qué?
But you're just like a brother to me.
You'd never respect me again if we did.
We're due in Euston in 5 minutes.
People would see the cable-car rocking.
I couldn't, not in my own bed.
I'm not that sort of girl.
I'd miss the bus.

STUPIDEST ATTEMPT TO IMPRESS A FIRST DATE

When James Dyer met Audrey Plummer at The Dapper
Duck near Frinton, they immediately hit it off and
decided to go out dancing together at the Cat's Whisker
Nitespot. 'In the course of our conversation,' Dyer was
later to tell a court, 'I discovered that one of the
qualities that excited her most in a man was instant
problem solving.'

Soon the couple had their instant problem – Dyer
was refused entry to the Cat's Whisker since he was
wearing jeans and no tie. He asked Audrey Plummer
to wait for a moment, walked around the corner,
lobbed a brick through the front window of a clothes
shop and reappeared in a three piece suit, silk shirt
and dayglo bow tie.

The police arrived as the couple were sitting down
to dinner. The next day James Dyer proposed to Audrey

Plummer when she visited him in prison. She told reporters that she was 'thinking it over'.

HARSHEST CRITIC OF LORD PORN'S SEXUAL ACHIEVEMENTS

The permissive society found a surprising ally in July 1971, when the Reverend Anthony Hart-Synnot wrote in his parish magazine that promiscuous individuals with sexual irregularities did significantly less harm to society than people who have large families.

Anti-pornography campaigners who flaunted their family lives as if they were badges of respectability were singled out for particular criticism. 'Lord Longford is the father of eight children,' wrote the vicar, 'a sexual achievement more harmful to the community than any number of dirty books.'

MOST SHOCKING DEBAUCHEE

The Earl of Rochester (1648–1680) packed a lot of living into his thirty-two years. A heroic soldier in the Dutch Wars, he was expelled several times from the court of Charles II for dissolute behaviour – an achievement in itself – and wrote many poems, which enjoyed a *succes de scandale* at the time.

The nearest he came to writing an autobiographical work was thought to be 'The Debauch'e':

I rise at Eleven, I dine about Two,
I get drunk befor Sev'n; and the next Thing I do
I send for my whore, when for fear of a Clap,
I fuck in her hand, and I spew in her Lap;
Then we quarrel and scold, 'till I fall asleep,
When the Bitch growing bold, to my Picket does creep;
Then slily she leaves me, and t'revenge the Affront
At once she bereaves me of Money and Cunt.
If by Chance then I wake, hot-headed and drunk
What a Coil do I make for the loss of my Punk?
I storm and I roar, and I fall in Rage,
And missing my Whore, I bugger my Page.
Then crop-stick all Morning, I rail at my men,
And in Bed I lie yawning 'till Eleven again.

Tragically this and other Rochester poems were for many generations deemed to be too obscene to be published and have only been publicly available in recent years.

MOST SURPRISING GANG-BANG

A keen baseball fan, Mr Bob Sower, an entomologist from Oregon who was working on an artificial sex attractant for tussock moths, went straight to the local game from his laboratory.

As the match progressed, Sower became the object of amorous attention from millions of tussock moths and had to be rescued by other spectators.

One of his rescuers told the press, 'He was like a puffball. When we managed to get through to him, his suit was quite eaten away and half his hair was gone.'

BUSIEST CULT

There are some Tantric cults within Hinduism that believe that ritual sexuality is the height of religious sexuality and that, with the right kind of sexual experience, a man can achieve union with the godhead. In this state, all differences in the human condition become the same and the couple making love is able to understand the whole cosmic process.

For the sects, promiscuity is an act of religious devotion, and it has particular significance if the two partners are breaking through conventional morality.

So the least spiritually valuable act is with a wife and should only take place for the sake of procreation. After that, a man's salvation lies in sleeping with the following types of women, listed in order of religious merit: another man's wife, a virgin, a woman of a different caste, a prostitute, a member of his immediate family and a demoness. The final step towards adepthood is to sleep with the goddess herself.

GROOVIEST PARSON

Father John Hester, the vicar of St Anne's, Soho, and author of *Soho is my Parish*, was used to visiting his flock in strip clubs and massage parlours. Even so, he was touched and surprised to be asked to christen an entire strip troupe of fifteen girls as urgently as possible. Sadly, the girls group conversion had something to do with the fact that they were due to leave for a tour of Egypt the next day and they needed proof that they weren't Jewish.

Commenting on his work, Father Hester said, 'Striptease can give us an insight into beauty as can a Bach cantata or a glass of vintage claret.'

MOST REVEALING INSIGHT INTO THE FILM INDUSTRY

During the 1960s, a notoriously randy and gay film producer bought rights to an obviously unfilmable novel set in a boys' public school. Auditions of keen young actors, looking for parts in the film continued for month after month with no sign of a filming date being fixed, until eventually a friend asked him why on earth he had bought the rights.

'I thought of it like a pension,' the producer explained. 'It was to ensure that I'd have a little something coming in each week for the rest of my life.'

DODGIEST MARRIAGE PROSPECT

'A good wife should have mystery, magic, adventure, daredevil and be between 100 and 120 pounds and be under twenty . . . Women get crafty in their twenties,' the Reverend Glynne Wolfe, a seventy-six-year-old Baptist minister from California told *Sun Day* magazine. Wolfe feels that he is uniquely qualified to give his opinion since he has been married twenty-six times – so far.

In addition to his many ex-wives, the minister also

has twenty-two sons and eighteen daughters, aged between three and sixty-three, having first become a father at the age of thirteen.

Asked why all twenty-six marriages had ended in divorce, Wolfe explained that each of his wives proved to have some significant flaw. One had a family that disapproved of him, one was in her thirties when they married, one ate sunflower seeds in bed while watching television, and so on. The most common problem is his wives' reluctance to wake up at 5 am every morning, which is the Rev. Wolfe's favourite time to make love.

Wolfe is modest about his success. 'If I can get them young and dumb enough, I can teach them how to have fun. I'm cute, a gentleman in the lounge, a cook in the kitchen and a Romeo in the bedroom . . . Of course, I always have whisky in the house. A large one is the best pant remover I know of.'

Early in 1985, the Rev. Wolfe was in the Frank Sinatra wing of the Palm Springs Hospital, getting straightened out before his quest for wife no. 27. He has had his prostate sorted out, his cataracts removed and his hair tinted. 'I'm fit and ready, and desperately searching for a lasting marriage. I've made a few mistakes, but each time I thought it was forever.'

BROADEST DEFINITION OF 'SPARE PART'

Explaining why he continued to have an affair with a girl who he knew was being unfaithful to him, Kenneth Pegg told St Albans Crown Court that he had only seen her when her car had broken down and she needed him to bring round a spare part.

'As I was leaving, she threw her arms around me and started to cry. I put my arms around her simply to comfort her. She then pulled my trousers down. It seemed a display of affection.'

LEAST CONVENTIONAL SNOOKER TECHNIQUE

A Mrs Masters from Carshalton had been suspicious of her husband's behaviour for some time and, by dint of some careful snooping when she had pretended to be going out for the evening, she was convinced that she now had her proof. 'When I heard Robert making his usual I-am-reaching-sexual-climax sound, I flung back the curtains, and got them in the act.'

Mr Masters denied that anything improper had been going on between him and his dancing partner, Miss Carole Croxley. His explanation went as follows:

'I had moved the snooker table into the bedroom for greater elbow room. The noise my wife heard was merely an expression of my delight at having potted the black. The same excitement accounts for the fact that my wig was askew. As for why Miss Croxley had her trousers off – well, she had split the side seam while executing a backhand shot only a few minutes before my wife made her astonishing entry.'

Asked why they were playing in the dark, Mr Masters explained, 'We were concentrating, and sunset passed unnoticed.'

FASTEST-MOVING MILLIONAIRE

A millionaire ranch-owner flying from New York to Hong Kong spent the entire flight telling one of the stewardesses how attracted he was to her. When the plane landed, he kissed her and asked if she would marry him. The stewardess agreed to think it over.

She didn't take long to make up her mind. Remembering that he was due to fly out the next day, she radioed her acceptance to the plane as it flew out.

A duty stewardess on the flight deck took the call. 'Too late,' she said. 'I've just accepted him.'

ROCK STAR MOST SUSCEPTIBLE TO JAIL BAIT

In the late fifties and early sixties, Chuck Berry's career suffered a serious setback owing to his penchant for under-age girls.

He was arrested twice in 1959 – first when a fourteen-year-old Apache girl whom Berry had brought back from New Mexico, employed at his club and subsequently fired, grassed on him to the police; and secondly when he tried to pick up a young white girl in Mississippi.

The girl later confessed that she had been a prostitute and that her claim that Berry had 'compelled, induced and incited her to give herself up to debauchery' was a trifle exaggerated. Nonetheless, Berry was sent to prison and was unable to resume his career until 1964.

WORST LOSER

Proof that the idea of Gallic charm is a myth encouraged by generations of wily Frenchmen exists in the behaviour of William the Conqueror. The hero of the Norman Conquest apparently wooed women with the same degree of tenderness and warmth that he accorded the Anglo-Saxons. Having been rejected by Matilda, whom he had decided he should marry, he went to Bruges, lay in wait for her outside a church she was attending and, when she came out, seized her, beat her and kicked her, finally leaving her semi-conscious on the ground. When she had recovered, she consented to become queen.

SILLIEST LOVE MACHINE

Tired of recounting the sexual exploits of Warren Beatty, Ryan O'Neal and Prince Andrew, the *News of the World* devoted a 'super sexclusive' to the exploits of the man they called 'the Pint-Sized Romeo known in clubland circles as the Love Machine'. He is Chris Quinten who plays a garage mechanic in *Coronation Street*.

The article reveals the subtleties of Chris's seduction technique. Among his favourite tricks are:

- wearing built-up heels to conceal the fact that he's 5'7".
- assuming a false Jack-the-lad cockney accent, although he comes from Middlesbrough.
- when he gets his girl for the night home, stripping off his shirt and going into a series of body-

building exercises and push-ups before leading her to his king-sized bed. 'After a workout, I'm at my best in bed,' he told reporters.

While the *News of the World* found a number of girls to testify that he is the most embarrassing wally ever to sport a medallion, Chris was anxious to explain his technique to readers. 'As a gymnast, I know a lot about bodies,' he said modestly. 'You could say that I know how to press all the right buttons.'

STRONGEST CASE FOR GETTING STEAMED UP

A legal precedent was established by an Italian supreme court in March 1985 when it ruled that a couple making love in a car that has its windows steamed up is not guilty of public indecency.

The appeal case before the court concerned a teenage couple caught making love in a car in the centre of Turin. But the police pointed out that, when surveillance of the couple began, they were clearly visible – it was only about ten minutes later that the windows became steamed up and the police moved in.

The case caused considerable comment in the Italian press. Not only did it cast new light on police procedure but it was reported the couple had been at it in a Fiat 500, a feat previously thought to be physically impossible.

121 LEAST ROMANTIC PROPOSALS

'I was an ugly child,' said Mr Masib Nasution of North Sumatra, when asked by a court to explain why he had married 121 times and made a fortune from dowries. 'As I grew older, the ugliness increased. By the time I was thirty, many people considered me to be hideous. Then I met this witch Mrs Jima Oto. Her advice to me was to take up smoking and when I was about to propose – just blow the smoke in my beloved's eyes. I followed her words and that is why I am here today.'

MOST APTLY NAMED DEFENDANT

A woman accused of 'lewd and wanton behaviour' in the lobby, some guest-rooms and the gentlemen's toilet of the Gemini Hotel in Providence, Rhode Island, found herself on the front page of the local paper the next day. Her name was Lynda Whynot.

SHORTEST LIVED MARITAL BLISS

Moses Alexander, aged 93, and Mrs Frances Tompkins, aged 105, were married in Bata, New York, on 11 June 1831. The next day, they were both found dead in bed.

LEAST ATTRACTIVE STAGE ACT

Many rock stars have admitted the sexual thrill that performance provides but few have put it as succinctly as American seventies' star Patti Smith did.

'When I'm on the road,' she said, 'it means I'm away from somebody I love. It might mean I'm alone for the night, it might mean I'm not going to be making love for a month ... All I know is that in some moment every night I'm so committed that I piss myself or I come on stage – once I even shat myself on stage.'

ELEVEN

INTERNATIONAL 'IT'S A COCK-UP'

'What the gods call love and men
    adultery
Is much more common where the
    climate's sultry.'

Lord Byron

AUSTRALIA

Out for a walk in the countryside near Melbourne, Miss Marlene Travers was astonished to see a strange light in the sky. It was a UFO – a silver disc from which, after it landed near her, a tall handsome alien emerged. He transfixed her with his eyes and she knew that she was without a will of her own. Days later, she discovered that she was pregnant.

'Believe it or not,' she later told reporters, 'I was held captive in a flying saucer, raped and made pregnant by a man from outer space.'

CHINA

A French woman tourist emerging naked from her bath in a Shanghai hotel was confronted by an embarrassed room-boy who had entered with a pass-key. Later in the day she received an official complaint from a local Communist Party official. 'It is not permitted to be naked in the hotel room, only in the bathroom.'

When the tourist asked, with more than a hint of sarcasm, whether the boy had recovered, she was told that he was considerably upset and had been sent home to rest.

FRANCE

A magistrates court in Nice was recently told why M. Philippe Dannat had come to knock M. Georges David unconscious.

Dannat was with his wife and David was with a large blonde woman when they first met at a wife-swapping party near St Tropez. The blonde, David had told Dannat, 'only becomes excited when she sees me making love with someone else. Then you can do what you like with her.' Dannat eagerly stood back and he and the blonde watched while David made love to his wife.

'But when my turn came,' Dannat told the court, 'I discovered that the huge blonde was not Mme David but a huge rubber doll. I completely lost my temper.'

GABON

A crackdown on prostitution in Libreville was recently announced by President Omar Bongo of Gabon. Prostitutes were to be rounded up by police and 'given to the troops'.

'When they have had five or six soldiers on top of them, these women will understand that you mustn't street-walk in Gabon,' the President said.

178

HOLLAND

Asked by a judge why his client, a Dutch optician called Igor Bassman, had insisted on his women patients taking off their clothes and dancing around the room while he played the accordion, the defence lawyer explained this test was carried out to make sure that they were the right kind for contact lenses. 'My client received training in Great Britain where the practice is widespread,' he said.

INDIA

'Birth control is ruining our trade,' said Mr Dilban Khwaja of Uttar Pradesh, India, while announcing a campaign by the region's eunuchs against all forms of sterilization. He went on to explain that the eunuchs make a living by being hired out by parents to celebrate the birth of their children.

'We have composed a cycle of anti-sterilization songs that we are singing at marches – free,' said Mr Khwaja. 'We are also in contact with the Pope – a valuable ally to our cause.'

IRELAND

'We have been inundated,' said Tim O'Brien, a spokesman for The Irish Society for the Abolition of Sex, after advertisements had been placed in British local papers, promising an entirely sex-free vacation at holiday camps in Croagh Patrick, Ballymurphy and the Curragh.

Among the attractions on offer were 'nettle-whipping', duckings in ice-cold water and a mud-wrestling championship. Discipline at the camps, it was promised, would be harsh.

'People are fed up with the so-called "Sun, sea and squelching" 18–35 holidays and we offer an ideal alternative,' said Mr O'Brien. 'Our holidays will be open to anyone who is resolutely opposed to sex.'

Asked what would happen if couples were found not to have been entirely sex-free, O'Brien commented that they would 'probably be disciplined in a way that the other campers think most suitable.'

ISRAEL

Explaining how a large number of women at Manahem Maternity Hospital had received a highly unconventional form of artificial insemination from gynaecologist Dr Vaclav, a hospital spokesman said, 'None of the women have suffered physical harm but all of them had a long and intimate examination by Dr Vaclav, the result of which appears to be that they did not get the semen that they expected to get. There have only been three complaints.'

ITALY

Sixty-two-year-old Giovanni Roval who claims to have made love to 3,000 women in a lifelong career as a gigolo, explained that he often gets gifts instead of money. 'The other day, someone gave me a second-hand Morris Minor,' he said proudly.

JAPAN

The Takamatsu Photo Library was astonished at the response it received from eager amateur photographers after it had announced that five 'any pose considered' nude models would be present on an artistic cruise on the *Grace Maru* steam launch. No less than ten extra models had to be hired after the bookings had come in.

But so effective were the models' poses that soon after the trip had begun many of the six hundred photographers became as the *Japan Times* later put it, 'vehement'.

A small section however were appalled at what was being photographed and a disagreement ensued. Those who wished the 'any pose considered' session to continue took over the wheelhouse and the engine room to ensure that they wouldn't be short-changed.

The other group, claiming that they were 'utterly revolted', responded by throwing two of the nude models overboard. Thereupon those still photographing angrily threw the killjoys over the side after the models.

The mêlée ended when the launch capsized, ruining millions of yen worth of camera equipment. Over half the passengers were arrested as they stepped off the lifeboat.

NEW ZEALAND

Bookings for Air New Zealand flights were said to have shown 'a significant increase' following the highly-publicised suspension of one of their steward-esses.

During an eventful flight from Auckland to Hono-lulu, the girl had enlivened proceedings by running up and down the aisle of the plane with her skirt around her waist and waving her pants over her head, climbing on top of a sleeping male passenger and, having failed to wake him, dragging another passenger off to the toilet where she raped him.

Apparently other crew members had not noticed anything unusual about the girl's behaviour until the 'assistance required' signal started flashing outside the loo. Breaking in they found the stewardess and her victim. He had been thrown against the distress button by his over-enthusiastic partner.

NIGERIA

Since it was raining, Miss Mendele, a student from Wani, Nigeria, accepted a lift from Professor Gabriel Odigo. The girl asked about the strange 'DO NOT KISS

ME' sign in the back window of the car and the professor explained that he was a disabled driver and that this was a safety measure.

A court was later told that Miss Medele had agreed to accompany Professor Odigo to his room 'to study some papers that interested us both'. There he tried to kiss her.

'When I reminded him about his "DO NOT KISS ME" sign,' Miss Medele explained, 'he said it was to stop people denting his bumper. So I told him that I would grant his request if he would take the sticker out of his car. He said he would do so, as soon as he left the room, I made my escape.'

Summing up, the magistrate agreed that Miss Medele had acted deceitfully but that was no justification for the professor to go round to her hostel and throw his artificial leg through the window.

SINGAPORE

After years of research, a team of doctors in Singapore have come up with the answer to one of life's great mysteries – what makes a man attractive? The answer is flat feet.

'In attracting the opposite sex, a flat-footed man is a phenomenon,' said Dr Gerard de Cordoisa. 'If you see a man surrounded by beautiful women, even if he is squat, balding and pot-bellied, the chances are he has flat feet.'

The doctor declined to comment on the state of his own feet.

SOUTH AFRICA

When a white South African businessman got into difficulties while swimming off a beach near Cape Town, a black kitchen maid, seeing his plight from a nearby road, dived in and dragged him, unconscious but alive, to the shore. But when she started giving the man the kiss of life, outraged whites on the beach pulled her off and took her to the nearest police station. The man died.

SOVIET UNION

Anxious to improve her sex life with her husband, a woman from Vinnitsa in the Soviet Union tried an exciting new technique that was, according to a friend of hers, very popular in the West – pulling her husband's testicles. The husband was later rushed to the casualty section of the local hospital, unconscious and in a state of shock.

SWEDEN

The backlash against permissiveness in Sweden has become so pronounced that there is now serious concern about the falling birth-rate.

The most dramatic evidence of the new puritanism is in the rapid spread of the so-called 'erotic-free zones'. The idea, which was pioneered at a hospital in Vastera, near Stockholm, involves painting a white line on the floor beyond which no one is permitted to have erotic thoughts about those around them. Doctors at the hospital, who had found that their work was suffering because of the sexual pressures put on them by nurses, have been enthusiastic supporters of the scheme. 'At last,' said Dr Bjorn Ahlstrom, head of the anaesthetic unit, 'we have a quiet corner where we can take refuge from all the meaningful, heavy glances and indecent suggestions.'

Men throughout Sweden, tired of the incessant demands of their womenfolk, have seized on the idea with gratitude. Many homes now have 'erotic-free zones' and the Swedish parliament is also now officially 'erotic-free'. A group has been set up dedicated to putting a white line around the whole of Stockholm, allowing one small area for those who wish to have erotic thoughts. Feminist groups have argued that this is an infringement of basic liberties but the scheme has many influential male supporters throughout the country. 'Permissiveness has had its day here,' Gunnar Ravenas, a lawyer from Stockholm, told *Newsweek*. 'These erotic-free zones are like a life-line for the average Swedish man.'

TURKEY

There was confusion after twenty-five-year-old Sether Seniz, a belly-dancer, offered herself for 'three nights of ecstasy' to any player in Turkey's football team to score against West Germany in a crucial international game. 'I am making the offer,' Seniz told the press, 'so that our boys have a little bit more to fight for.'

Many later blamed Turkey's 4-0 defeat to the Germans on the publicity surrounding the affair. Turkish backs had protested that, as defenders, they were less likely to score and the captain, who was goalkeeper, argued strenuously that he should have 'captain's rights' if any of his team scored. A penalty awarded to Turkey was only taken after scuffles among the players and was then missed.

The West German soccer authorities having complained to the Turks about what they called, 'the most unique form of doping known to sport', were relieved to see how badly the incentive had backfired.

After the match, one German player remarked that he had considered scoring an own goal, but, after seeing a photograph of Sether Seniz, had changed his mind.

UNITED KINGDOM

The Amberwood Hotel in Devon, according to the *Sex Maniac's Diary 1985*, is the first hotel in Britain to openly invite swingers as guests. However, the invitation is regrettably only open to the middle-aged swinger 'because younger couples remind guests of their children'.

UNITED STATES

A bizarre new twist to America's sex-on-the-phone craze has been revealed by the trial in New York of Kenneth Cohen, vice president of a TV marketing company.

Cohen was said to have phoned women posing as their husband's psychiatrists. He would then explain that their husbands were on the verge of suicide – and only if their sexual fantasies involving their nearest and dearest were satisfied would they be saved.

The fantasies usually involved the wives bringing lovers into the house, making love to them, later phoning the 'psychiatrist' to tell him all the details. Above all, the affairs were never to be discussed with their husbands.

Cohen's calls are said to have fooled hundreds of women, many of whom called on their neighbours or found strangers on the street to help save their husbands. One wife in Teaneck, New Jersey, took her gardener away from his mowing and spent the whole afternoon with him, so urgent was her husband's problem.

WALES

A Welsh psychologist has claimed that, if women – as it has been claimed – sublimate their sexual needs by watching soap operas on the television; men get the same kind of charge out of watching televised sport.

'No one who has seen a group of men watching wrestling or a scrumdown at a rugby match could deny that there is something very definitely sexual about it,' he commented.

WEST GERMANY

On the wedding night of a German couple from Hiessen, the groom, aged seventy-three, decided to make an early night of it and retired to bed at 9 pm to read the Bible. He was still reading at 2 am in the morning when his bride, aged fifty-three, disturbed him by leaping up and down stark naked at the end of his bed.

Terrified by this spectacle, the man threw his Bible at her and jumped out of the window into eight feet of snow. The bride followed him, still in a state of undress, and pursued him around the town until, two hours later, they were both arrested for causing a disturbance.

YUGOSLAVIA

Called out to repair the kitchen sink at the house of a newly married couple, Yugoslavian plumber Miodrag Jacic was let into the house by the husband, who then went out to do some shopping.

When the wife came home, she noticed two legs sticking out from under the sink and, thinking they belonged to her husband, decided to give him a pleasant surprise of an oral nature. The plumber was so startled by what then happened that he hit his head on the sink above him and was concussed.

An ambulance was called and, as he was being taken down the steps, one of the ambulance men asked what exactly had happened. The answer amused him so much that he dropped the stretcher breaking Jacic's arm.

The plumber threatened to sue the couple while the wife was reported to be so traumatized by the incident for several weeks she refused to speak to her husband.

ZIMBABWE

Giving evidence in the trial of Mr Magenga Josiah, a Zimbabwean policeman, for rape, the victim, who has admitted she was a prostitute, told the court that the alleged incident took place under some bushes. 'I don't understand why he raped me,' she said. 'If he had asked properly, I would have only charged him 2/6d.'

THE EROTIC FAILURES
HALL OF FAME

THE EROTIC FAILURES
HALL OF FAME

The following celebrities have been elected to the Hall of Fame having each earned an honourable mention in *The Book of Erotic Failures* or *More Erotic Failures*:

William Acton
St Mary Marie Alacoque
Al Alvarez
Mrs Al Alvarez
Aly Khan
Ian Anderson
Princess Anne
Queen Anula of Ceylon
St Thomas Aquinas
Debee Ashby
Robin Askwith

Honoré de Balzac
Countess Elizabeth Bathay
Charles Baudelaire
Warren Beatty (×2)
Samuel Beckett
Chuck Berry
Jim Bishop
Tony Blackburn (×2)
Easy Blow
Chay Blyth
Cesare Borgia
President Bourguiba of Tunisia
Clara Bow
Lord Bradwell (×2)

Marlon Brando
Sir Thomas Browne
Robert Browning
Anthony Burgess
Sir Richard Burton (×3)

Dyan Cannon
Jonathan Cape
Truman Capote
Casanova
Lord Castlehaven
Lady Castlehaven
Charles II
Dr Robert Chartham
Queen Christina of Sweden
Lewis Collins
Sir Dennis Compton
Shirley Conran
Jilly Cooper
Harry Corbett
King Cotys of Thrace
Joan Crawford
Aleister 'The Great Beast' Crowley

Sammy Davis Jnr (×3)
Dr David Delvin
J. P. Donleavy
Bob Dylan

Edward VIII
George Eliot
Duke Ellington
Chevalier d'Eon de Beaumont
Kenny Everett
Lee Everett

Felix Fauré
F. Scott Fitzgerald

Marvin Gaye
Boy George
Dana Gillespie
Al Goldstein
Johann Goethe
Cary Grant
Germaine Greer

'Diddy' David Hamilton
Frederick Hankey
Jean Harlow
Maria Harper
Frank Harris
Jim Haynes
Emperor Heliogabalus
Ernest Hemingway (×2)
Adolf Hitler
J. Edgar Hoover
Dennis Hopper
Rock Hudson
Howard Hughes
Victor Hugo

Mick Jagger (×3)
Henry James
Tom Jones
Erica Jong

Mustafa Kunt

Hedy Lamarr
Larry the Lonely Policeman
D. H. Lawrence
Frieda Lawrence
Lynda Lee-Potter
Jack Lemmon
Liberace
Little Richard

'Dirty' Dai Llewellyn
Gina Lollobrigida
Lord Longford
Linda Lovelace (×2)
Martin Luther

Madame de Maintenon
Barry Manilow
The 10th Duke of Marlborough
H. L. Mencken
King Menephta of Egypt
Gitty Milinaire
Congressman Wilbur Mills
Lord Milton
Jim Morrison

Emperor Napoleon
Ilie Nastase
Emperor Nero
Florence Nightingale
Anais Nin
David Niven (×2)
Jeff Nuttall

Phil Oakley
Merle Oberon
Onan
Ryan O'Neal (×3)
Donny Osmond
Peter O'Toole

Cecil Parkinson MP
Françoise Pascal
Michelle Philips
General Plastiras

Chris Quinten
Sultan Qutb-ud-din of Gujarat

Bagwan Shree Rajneesh
Debbie Reynolds
The Earl of Rochester (×2)
Johnny Rotten

King Ibn Saud of Saudi Arabia
Peter Sellers
Omar Sharif (×2)
Artie Shaw
Frank Sinatra
Denis Skinner MP
Patti Smith
Valerie Solanas
Dr Benjamin Spock
Rod Stewart
Jacqueline Susann
Algernon Swinburne

Margaret Thatcher MP
J. R. 'Chuck' Traynor

Evelyn Waugh
Lord Wigoder
Toyah Wilcox
Kim Wilde
William the Conqueror
Heathcote Williams
Tennessee Williams
Wendy O. Williams and the Plasmatics
Virginia Woolf

ACKNOWLEDGEMENTS

Many of the erotic failures in this book were plundered from the pages of the British press, in particular the *Guardian*, the *Daily Mirror*, the *Daily Star*, the *Sun*, *The Times*, the *Daily Mail*, the *Mail on Sunday*, the *News of the World*, the *Sunday Mirror*, the *New Statesman*, *Company*, *Revue*, *Forum* and, above all, *Private Eye*, whose wonderful 'True Stories' column was a rich source of disasters.

I am indebted to the helpful staff at the Colindale Newspaper Library, the British Library, the *Daily Mirror* Reference Library and the New York Public Library.

Above all, thanks should go to Jenny and Rowena Prior, both of whom now know considerably more about erotic failure than is strictly seemly or healthy.

BIBLIOGRAPHY

Alan Bestic, *Sex and the Singular English* (Taplinger, 1972)

William A. Brend, *Sacrifice to Attis* (Heinemann, 1936)

Vern L. Bullough, *Sexual Variance in Society and History* (John Wiley, 1976)

Abigail van Buren, *Dear Abby* (Prentice Hall, 1958)

Bob Chieger, *Was It Good For You Too?* (Arrow, 1984)

Albert Ellis, *Sex Beliefs and Customs* (Peter Nevill, 1952)

Nina Epton, *Love and the English* (Cassell, 1960)

Ross Firestone, *A Book of Men* (Mainstream, 1979)

Jim Haynes, *Thanks For Coming!* (Faber and Faber, 1984)

Gary Herman, *Rock 'n' Roll Babylon* (Plexus, 1982)

David Lewis, *Sexpionage* (John Wiley, 1976)

Margaret Nicholas, *The World's Wickedest Women* (Octopus, 1984)

Joseph R. Orgel, *Undying Passion* (Morrow, 1985)

Tuppy Owens, *The Sex Maniac's Diary 1985* (Owens, 1985)

Ronald Pearsall, *Public Purity, Private Shame* (Weidenfeld, 1976)

Amy Richlin, *The Garden of Priapus* (Yale University Press, 1983)

Amoury de Riencourt, *Sex and Power in History* (McKay, 1974)

Gary Rimmer, *Lonely Hearts* (Unwin Paperbacks, 1983)

Penny Stallings, *Rock 'n' Roll Confidential* (Vermilion, 1984)

Dr Michael Stern and Dr August Stern, *Sex in the Soviet Union* (W. H. Allen, 1981)

John Train, *Remarkabilia* (Allen and Unwin, 1984)

Michael Turner and Michael Geare, *Gluttony, Pride and Lust* (Collins, 1984)

Amy Wallace, David Wallechinsky and Irving Wallace, *The Book of Lists 3* (Elm Tree, 1983)

Charles White, *The Life and Times of Little Richard* (Pan, 1985)

Alan Wykes, *Eccentric Doctors* (Mowbrays, 1975)

THE BOOK OF MISTAIKES

Gyles Brandreth

'English shorthand typist. Efficien. Useless. Apply otherwise.'
ADVERTISEMENT IN A SPANISH NEWSPAPER

'The ladies of St Martin's Church have discarded clothing of all kinds. Call at 152 North Street for inspection. Mrs Freeman will be willing to oblige you in any way she can.'
Worthing Gazette

'On making enquiries at the Hospital this afternoon, we learn that the deceased is as well as can be expected.'
Jersey Evening Post

THE BOOK OF MISTAIKES

An amazing mixture of misprints, misnomers and misunderstandings . . . a collection of classic clangers, hilarious howlers and headlines gone haywire . . . a dictionary of disaster ranging from the decidedly dreadful to the definitely delightful.

Futura Publications
Humour
0 7088 2194 4

YOU FAT SLOB

Anthony Palmer

If your F-Plan didn't go according to plan, and the
Beverly Hills Diet made no impression on your
mountains of flab –
GIVE UP THE FADS AND GET RID OF THE FAT
RELY ON YOURSELF

Anthony Palmer – 15½ years, 18½ stone – did, and
now he's got a lot less of himself to rely on.

This is his diary; a hilarious and personal record of
his determined efforts to become less like the
Michelin Man and more like Clint Eastwood, by
eating imaginary Jaffa Cakes, guzzling milk shakes
(yes, really!) and braving the horrors of unisex
aerobics. There is also a section of mouth-watering,
but flab-fighting, menus and special diets.

Futura Publications
Non-fiction
0 7088 2653 9

THE BOOK OF EXCUSES

Gyles Brandreth

A COMPLETE GUIDE TO HOW TO COME UP WITH THE PERFECT EXCUSE!

Whoever you are – a child who hasn't done his homework, a husband who arrives home later than expected, a secretary who never gets to the office on time, a zookeeper who can't persuade his pandas to breed – you need an excuse.

They don't always need to be elaborate, but they always ought to be convincing – and with Gyles Brandreth's entertaining guidance and his selection of the most amazing real-life excuses ever known – they certainly will be!

From the government spokesman who excused the fact that Britain had been left behind in the race to the moon on the grounds that we led the world in sewage treatment . . .

. . . to the Unigate milkman who told an industrial tribunal that the reason he joined the housewife in her bath was to help her rinse her empties . . .

. . . to an unemployed accountant who, when asked in court whether he had sold a £3 bag of manure for £650, replied: 'Mark-ups are normal in any profession.'

THE BOOK OF EXCUSES MEANS YOU'LL NEVER HAVE TO SAY SORRY AGAIN!

Futura Publications
Humour
0 7088 2452 8

CRITICS' GAFFES

Ronald Duncan

with cartoons by Gray Jolliffe

What did learned professors have to say about flying?
'Artificial flight is impossible.'

What did the papers say about the Gettysburg Address?
'. . . dull and commonplace . . .'

What did Rossini say about Wagner?
'. . . good moments but bad quarter-hours . . .'

And what did critics say about Picasso?
'. . . the most Godalmighty rubbish . . .'

In each case, they Got it Wrong – with a vengeance! Gathered here are the best and funniest mistakes made by experts who came a cropper, in every field of the arts and sciences. Gray Jolliffe's hilarious cartoons hammer home the nails in their self-made coffins.

Futura Publications
Non-fiction/humour
0 7088 2558 0

1984 AND ALL THAT

Paul Manning

THIS BOOK CHANGES HISTORY

A *Relevant* Guide to the 20th Century, containing 103 *Valid Insights*, 5 *Viable Hypostases* and many *Challenging Assertions*, ranging from the Broadly Tenable to the Purely Suppository

Did you know that:

German wartime propaganda was masterminded by gerbils?

Oswald Mosley invented a popular Swiss breakfast food?

Could you say how many currants are contained in an average slice of the National Cake?

Almost certainly the answer is No. Yet now at last these vital facts and many others can be at your fingertips, thanks to

1984 AND ALL THAT

– the indispensable history of the world since 1914 –

which boldly takes up where the classic 1066 AND ALL THAT left off, bringing you a mine of hilarious misinformation on everything from the Infernal Combustion Engine and the Nuclear Umbrella to the Gross National Product.

Culled from a lifetime's research in saloon bars up and down the country, ruthlessly purged of all Unhistorical or Irrelevant matter,

dare you be without it?

'An historical document of the first importance. I am convinced it is genuine.'
(with apologies to) Lord Dacre

Futura Publications
Fiction/Humour
0 7088 2612 1

All Futura Books are available at your bookshop or newsagent, or can be ordered from the following address:
Futura Books, Cash Sales Department,
P.O. Box 11, Falmouth, Cornwall.

Please send cheque or postal order (no currency), and allow 55p for postage and packing for the first book plus 22p for the second book and 14p for each additional book ordered up to a maximum charge of £1.75 in U.K.

Customers in Eire and B.F.P.O. please allow 55p for the first book, 22p for the second book plus 14p per copy for the next 7 books, thereafter 8p per book.

Overseas customers please allow £1 for postage and packing for the first book and 25p per copy for each additional book.